MARTIN CLASSICAL LECTURES

MARTIN CLASSICAL LECTURES

These lectures are delivered annually at

OBERLIN COLLEGE

on a foundation established in honor of

CHARLES BEEBE MARTIN

The Classics and Renaissance Thought

MARTIN CLASSICAL LECTURES
VOLUME XV

BY

PAUL OSKAR KRISTELLER

PUBLISHED FOR OBERLIN COLLEGE

BY

HARVARD UNIVERSITY PRESS

CAMBRIDGE, MASSACHUSETTS

1955

LIBRARY OF CONGRESS CATALOG CARD NUMBER 55-9440
PRINTED IN THE UNITED STATES OF AMERICA
AT THE PRESS OF THE OBERLIN PRINTING COMPANY
OBERLIN, OHIO, U. S. A.

THE MARTIN CLASSICAL LECTURES

Volume XV

The Martin Foundation, on which these lectures are delivered, was established by his many friends in honor of Charles Beebe Martin, for forty-five years a teacher of classical literature and classical art in Oberlin College.

TO MY COLLEAGUES
AT COLUMBIA UNIVERSITY

PREFACE

I WISH to express my thanks and appreciation to my colleagues at Oberlin College who kindly invited me to deliver these lectures on February 22-26, 1954, and decided afterwards to have them published. I welcomed the opportunity thus offered me to present my views on a subject which has attracted me for many years and which, to my knowledge, has not been treated in any recent comprehensive study. I also feel somewhat hesitant to publish these views since I cannot prove or document them in such a short study, and since I happen to disagree with many distinguished scholars whose work I have yet every reason to respect.

The lectures are published here essentially as delivered, but I was kindly allowed to add a section of notes. I decided to use this space mainly to acquaint the more curious reader with those studies in which he may find further detail and evidence relevant to the various aspects of our subject.

To those of my readers who are primarily interested in philosophy and its history, I must apologize for the scarcity of doctrinal analysis. Within the limited time and space at my disposal, I felt that I would do more justice to my subject by trying to draw a rough but comprehensive map of Renaissance learning in some of its aspects, and thus to help prepare a system of orientation in which each thinker and each philosophical idea might eventually be assigned its proper historical place.

PAUL OSKAR KRISTELLER

Columbia University
August 13, 1954.

CONTENTS

THE CLASSICS AND
RENAISSANCE THOUGHT

1.   THE HUMANIST MOVEMENT

I GREATLY appreciate the honor of being invited to deliver the Martin Classical Lectures this year, and of being a guest of Oberlin College, an institution noted for its distinguished tradition in the humanities, and well known to Renaissance scholars for the outstanding work of its former president, Ernest Wilkins.   Ever since I myself received a training in classical philology and wrote my doctoral dissertation on a Greek philosopher, I have retained, in the face of the changing winds of fashionable opinion, a firm belief in the continuing value of classical studies and of a classical education.   Thus I have never failed, in my efforts to understand certain philosophical writers of the Renaissance period, to pay due attention to the influences exercised upon them by classical antiquity, and I greatly welcome this opportunity to present in a more comprehensive manner my views on this important subject, as fully as the available time and the state of my information will permit.

Since philosophical and historical no less than political discussions are apt to sink into confusion through the use of vague and ill-defined notions, and since I feel unable to speak about my subject without using some of the general terms traditionally applied to it, I should like to explain first how I plan to use some of these terms.

The meaning of the term "Renaissance" has been the subject of an unending controversy among recent historians, who have been debating about the value, the distinctive characteristics, the time limits, and the very existence of that historical period.[1]   I shall not repeat or refute any of the arguments proposed by others, but merely state that by "the Renaissance" I understand that period of Western European history which extends approximately from 1300 to 1600, without any preconception as to the characteristics or merits of that period, or of those periods preceding and following it. I do not pretend to assert that there was a sharp break at the beginning or end of "the Renaissance," or to deny that there was a good deal of continuity. I should even admit that in some respects the changes which occurred in the twelfth and thirteenth or in the seventeenth and eighteenth centuries were more profound than the changes of the fourteenth and fifteenth. I merely maintain that the so-called Renaissance period has a distinctive physiognomy of its own, and that the inability of historians to find a simple and satisfactory definition for it does not entitle us to doubt its existence; otherwise, by the same token, we should have to question the existence of the Middle Ages, or of the eighteenth century. The Renaissance is a very complex period and it encompassed, just as do the Middle Ages or any other period, a good many chronological, regional, and social differences. Not being able to do equal justice to all aspects of the Renaissance, I shall focus our attention, though not exclusively, upon Italy in the fifteenth and early sixteenth centuries. Whereas the cultural differences between Italy and Northern Europe were no less marked during the high Middle Ages than during the Renaissance, in the fifteenth century Italy, along with the Low Countries, attained a position of intellectual leadership in Western Europe which she had not possessed in the preceding age. If Europe during the Middle Ages had one or several Renaissances, as some scholars believe, Italy's share in these earlier "Renaissances" was rather limited. On the other hand, if the Renaissance of the fifteenth century, seen against the background of the French Middle Ages, does not appear to some historians like a rebirth of Europe, it certainly appeared to its contemporaries, against the background of the Italian Middle Ages, like a rebirth of Italy. Moreover, I shall not discuss the Renaissance in terms of a few outstanding and well-known

thinkers and writers alone, but I shall rather try to draw a
cultural map of the period, taking into account the vast
amount of information hidden away in the bibliographies of
early editions, in the collections and catalogues of manuscript books, and in the records of schools, universities, and
other learned institutions. This approach will enable us also
to view the great writers of the period in a better perspective, and to judge in each case whether we are dealing with
the representative expression of a broad trend of thinking,
or with the isolated and original contribution of an individual mind.

If we try to understand the thought and philosophy of
the Renaissance, or of any other period, we are of course
confronted with a variety of currents and of individual
writers, which defies any attempt at a general description.
The task becomes even more complex if we extend our view
beyond the area of "philosophy" in the narrow and technical
sense, characterized by professional traditions and the discipline of method, into the vast field of general thought embodied in the writings of poets and prose authors, of scholars, scientists, or theologians. To some extent the historian
of philosophy is driven to follow this course, since the very
meaning of philosophy, the emphasis it puts on certain problems, its relations to other fields of intellectual endeavor, the
place it occupies in the system of culture, are apt to undergo
a continuous change. On the other hand, our task is simpli-
fied in so far as we are not considering Renaissance thought
in its originality or in its entire content, but merely in its relation to classical antiquity.

This relation in turn calls for one further preliminary
remark. To be sure, the world of classical antiquity, and
especially its literature and philosophy, seems to possess a
solid reality which, like a high mountain range, has remained
above the horizon for many centuries. Yet on closer inspec-
tion, it becomes apparent that the use made of this heritage

by later generations has been subject to many changes. Each period has offered a different selection and interpretation of ancient literature, and individual Greek and Latin authors as well as their individual writings have seen more or less deep ebbs and tides of popularity at different times. Hence we shall not be surprised to learn that the Renaissance attitude towards classical antiquity differed in many ways from that of medieval or modern times. Modern classicism, which originated in the eighteenth century and continues to influence our approach to the classics, though it has been modified since then by various currents of historical, archaeological, and anthropological scholarship, has tended to focus our attention upon the literature and thought of the early and classical Greek period down to the fourth century B.C., and to a lesser degree upon Roman literature to the first century A.D.; whereas the later phases of Greek and Latin literature, and especially of its doctrinal and scientific literature, have been comparatively neglected. Medieval Europe, on the other hand, lived for many centuries in the direct tradition of Roman antiquity, used the Latin language as a medium for its learning and much of its literature and business, and knew some though not all of the ancient Roman poets and prose authors quite thoroughly, yet was with a few exceptions unfamiliar with the Greek language and with its classical literature. Moreover, the early Middle Ages, from the time of the Latin Church Fathers, were concerned with the problem of reconciling the study of the pagan classics with the teachings and commands of Christianity, a problem which received added urgency from the fact that the learning of the period was almost entirely in the possession of the Catholic clergy. During the later Middle Ages, and more specifically between the middle of the eleventh and the end of the thirteenth centuries, profound changes occurred in the intellectual culture of Western Europe. A growing professional interest developed in philosophy and in the sciences, which was kindled by Arabic influences and nourished by a flood of Latin translations, from the Arabic and from the Greek, through which many writings of Aristotle and of a few other Greek philosophers, of Euclid and Ptolemy, Galen and Hippocrates became for the first time available to Western students. This later medieval interest in the works of certain Greek philosophers and scientists must be clearly distinguished from the earlier medieval study of the classical Latin poets and prose writers. Actually, there was a conflict between the representatives of the *artes,* that is, of the liberal arts and the scientific and philosophical disciplines, and the followers of the *authores,* that is, of the great books, and by the thirteenth century the latter tendency had suffered a decisive, though perhaps temporary, defeat.[2] The Renaissance attitude towards the classics inherited some features from the Middle Ages, but was different from the earlier and later medieval approach, as well as from that of modern classicism. Renaissance scholars continued or resumed the study of the Latin authors that had been cultivated by the medieval grammarians, but greatly expanded and improved it, and also pursued it for its own sake. They were not anti-Christian, but as laymen they did not subordinate the development of secular learning to its amalgamation with religious or theological doctrine. Moreover, they added the study of the Greek language and of its entire literature, going far beyond the limits of science and of Aristotelian philosophy. Finally, guided by their enthusiasm for everything ancient, and by the conscious program of imitating and reviving ancient learning and literature, Renaissance scholars had a much more comprehensive interest in ancient literature than either medieval or modern students. They did not despise late or minor authors, and even accepted many apocryphal works as authentic. As a result of this broad interest, classical studies occupied in the Renaissance a more central place in the civilization of the period, and were more intimately linked with its other intellectual tendencies and achievements, than at any earlier or later time in the history of Western Europe.

If we are to understand the role of classical studies in the Renaissance, we must begin with the humanist movement. The term "Humanism" has been associated with the Renaissance and its classical studies for more than a hundred years, but in recent times it has become the source of much philosophical and historical confusion. In present discourse, almost any kind of concern with human values is called "humanistic," and consequently a great variety of thinkers, religious or antireligious, scientific or antiscientific, lay claim to what has become a rather elusive label of praise. We might ignore this twentieth-century confusion, but for the direct impact it has had upon historical studies. For many historians, knowing that the term "humanism" has been traditionally associated with the Renaissance, and seeing that some features of the modern notion of "humanism" seem to have their counterparts in the thought of that period, have cheerfully applied the term "humanism" in its vague modern meaning to the Renaissance and to other periods of the past, speaking of Renaissance humanism, medieval humanism, or Christian humanism, in a fashion which defies any definition and seems to have little or nothing left of the basic classicist meaning of Renaissance humanism.[3] This seems to me a bad example of that widespread tendency among historians to impose the terms and labels of our modern time upon the thought of the past. If we want to understand the philosophy of the Renaissance or of any other period, we must try not only to separate the interpretation of the authentic thought of the period from the evaluation and critique of its merits, but also to recapture the original meaning in which that period employed certain categories and classifications which either have become unfamiliar to us, or have acquired different connotations. In the case of the term "Humanism," its historical ancestry has become pretty clear as a result of recent studies. The term *Humanismus* was coined in 1808 by the German educator, F. J. Niethammer, to express the emphasis on the Greek and Latin classics in secondary education, as against the rising demands for a more practical and more scientific training.[4] In this sense, the word was applied by many historians of the nineteenth century to the scholars of the Renaissance, who had also advocated and established the central role of the classics in the curriculum, and who in some German cities had founded in the sixteenth century the same schools which were still carrying on that tradition in the nineteenth. The term *Humanismus,* in the specific sense of a program and ideal of classical education, cannot be dismissed on account of its comparatively recent origin. For it is derived from another similar word, "humanist," whose origin can be traced back to the Renaissance itself. *Humanista* in Latin, and its vernacular equivalents in Italian, French, English, and other languages, were terms commonly used in the sixteenth century for the professor or teacher or student of the humanities, and this usage remained alive and was well understood until the eighteenth century.[5] The word, to judge from its earliest appearance known so far, seems to have originated in the student slang of the Italian universities, where the professor of the humanities came to be called *umanista,* after the analogy of his colleagues in the older disciplines, to whom the terms *legista, jurista, canonista,* and *artista* had been applied for several centuries. The term *humanista,* coined at the height of the Renaissance period, was in turn derived from an older term, that is, from the "humanities" or *studia humanitatis.* This term was apparently used in the general sense of a liberal or literary education by such ancient Roman authors as Cicero and Gellius, and this use was resumed by the Italian scholars of the late fourteenth century.[6] By the first half of the fifteenth cen-

tury, the *studia humanitatis* came to stand for a clearly defined cycle of scholarly disciplines, namely grammar, rhetoric, history, poetry, and moral philosophy,[7] and the study
of each of these subjects was understood to include the reading and interpretation of its standard ancient writers in
Latin and, to a lesser extent, in Greek. This meaning of the
studia humanitatis remained in general use through the sixteenth century and later, and we may still find an echo of it
in our use of the term "humanities." Thus Renaissance
humanism was not as such a philosophical tendency or system, but rather a cultural and educational program which
emphasized and developed an important but limited area of
studies. This area had for its center a group of subjects that
was concerned essentially neither with the classics nor with
philosophy, but might be roughly described as literature. It
was to this peculiar literary preoccupation that the very in-
tensive and extensive study which the humanists devoted to
the Greek and especially to the Latin classics owed its peculiar character, which differentiates it from that of modern
classical scholars since the second half of the eighteenth century. Moreover, the *studia humanitatis* includes one philosophical discipline, that is, morals, but it excludes by definition such fields as logic, natural philosophy, and metaphysics,
as well as mathematics and astronomy, medicine, law, and
theology, to mention only such fields as had a firmly established place in the university curriculum and in the classifi-
cation schemes of the period. This stubborn fact seems to
me to provide irrefutable evidence against the repeated attempts to identify Renaissance humanism with the philosophy, the science, or the learning of the period as a whole.[8]
On the other hand, if we want to apply the Renaissance term
"humanist" to the medieval period, which did not use it, we
may choose to call "humanists" certain Carolingian scholars
such as Alcuin or Lupus of Ferrières, or certain twelfth-cen-
tury authors such as John of Salisbury or the grammarians

of Orléans and Chartres, on account of the affinity of their learned interests with those of the Italian humanists of the Renaissance. But if we call St. Thomas Aquinas a "humanist" because of his indebtedness to the Greek philosopher Aristotle, we might as well apply the same label to all other Aristotelian philosophers of the later Middle Ages, and also to all medieval mathematicians, astronomers, medical authors, or jurists, on account of their dependence upon such ancient authorities as Euclid, Ptolemy, Galen, or the Corpus Juris; and thus we shall have deprived ourselves of a very helpful distinction indeed. Hence I should like to ask you to keep the Renaissance meaning of "humanities" and "humanist" well in mind whenever I use the term "humanism" in these lectures, and to forget our modern uses of the word as completely as you can. If you fail to do so, I cannot be held responsible for the resulting confusion.

The central importance of literary preoccupations in Renaissance humanism might be illustrated by the professional status of the humanists, most of whom were active either as teachers of the humanities in secondary schools or universities, or as secretaries to princes or cities, and by the bulk of their extant writings, which consist of orations, letters, poems, and historical works and which are in part still unpublished or even unsifted. It cannot be our task in this lecture to give an account of these professional activities of the humanists, or of their contributions to Neolatin literature and to the various vernacular literatures. I merely want to point out that Renaissance humanism must be understood as a characteristic phase in what may be called the rhetorical tradition in Western culture. This tradition is as old as the Greek Sophists, and it is very much alive in our own day, although the word "rhetoric" has become distasteful to many people. For the studies of speech and composition, of English and creative writing, of advertisement and business correspondence are nothing but modern varieties of the age-old rhetorical enterprise that tries to teach oral and written expression by means of rules and models. Since the rhetorician offers to speak and to write about everything, and the philosopher tries to think about everything, they have always been rivals in their claim to provide a universal training of the mind. This rivalry appeared in Plato's polemic against the Sophists; it continued throughout the later centuries of Greek antiquity in the competing schools of the philosophers and of the rhetoricians,[9] it was largely forgotten among the Romans and their successors in the early Middle Ages, for the simple reason that they had a strong rhetorical, but no philosophical, tradition; it reappeared in various ways in the high Middle Ages with the rise of philosophical studies,[10] and again in the Renaissance when humanistic learning began to compete with the scholastic tradition of Aristotelian philosophy. The relation between the two traditions has been complicated by the fact that the rhetoricians ever since Isocrates have been concerned with morals and have liked to call themselves philosophers, whereas the philosophers ever since Aristotle have tended to offer their own version of rhetoric as a part of philosophy. The historical significance of rhetoric cannot be fully understood unless we take into consideration not only the rhetorical theories of philosophers such as Aristotle and his scholastic successors, or of rhetoricians who tried to combine rhetoric and philosophy such as Cicero, but also the rhetoric of the rhetoricians, that is, of the authors professionally concerned with the practice of speaking and writing. In medieval Italy, this profession was strongly represented from the late eleventh century on by the so-called *dictatores* who taught and practiced, on the basis of textbooks and models, the eminently practical art of composing documents, letters, and public speeches.[11] It has become clear as a result of recent investigation that the humanists of the Renaissance were the professional successors of the medieval Italian *dictatores,* and inherited from them the various patterns of epistolography and public oratory, all more or less determined by the customs and practical needs of later medieval society. Yet the medieval *dictatores* were no classical scholars and used no classical models for their compositions. It was the novel contribution of the humanists to add the firm belief that in order to write and to speak well it was necessary to study and to imitate the ancients. Thus we can understand why classical studies in the Renaissance were rarely, if ever, separated from the literary and practical aim of the rhetorician to write and to speak well. This practical and professional connection provided a strong incentive towards classical studies and helped to supply for them the necessary manpower for their proper development. For I cannot help feeling that the achievements of a given nation or period in particular branches of culture depend not only on individual talents, but also on the available professional channels and tasks into which these talents can be drawn and for which they are trained. This is a subject to which cultural and social historians apparently have not yet paid sufficient attention.

If we try to survey the contributions of the Renaissance humanists to classical scholarship, it will be helpful to distinguish between the Latin and the Greek fields. In the field of Latin studies, there was a much closer connection with the rhetorical and practical interests just mentioned, and also with the scholarly traditions of the Middle Ages, although we should keep in mind that these traditions had been less cultivated in Italy, the cradle of Renaissance humanism, than in the Northern countries, and had suffered a decline even in France during the period immediately preceding the Renaissance. Most attention has been paid to the humanist discoveries of classical Latin authors unknown or neglected during the Middle Ages.[12] The merit of these discoveries has been unduly disparaged with the remark that the manuscripts found by the humanists were written during the Middle Ages, and that the respective authors were consequently not unknown or in need of a discovery. If an ancient Latin text survived only in one or two Carolingian manuscripts, and if there are but scanty traces of its having been read during the subsequent centuries, the fact that such a text was found by a humanist and made generally available through numerous copies does constitute a discovery. On the other hand, the fact that some classical Latin authors such as Vergil or Ovid or Seneca or Boethius were widely known throughout the Middle Ages does not refute the equally obvious fact that some other authors such as Lucretius or Tacitus or Manilius were discovered by the humanists. It would be wrong to maintain that classical Latin literature as a whole was neglected during the Middle Ages, or to deny that a certain nucleus of it was commonly studied. It would be equally wrong to deny that as a result of the humanist discoveries the available patrimony of Latin literature was extended almost to its present limits, and that the writings added to the medieval nucleus included, besides less important texts, also some that have been important and influential. Moreover, the case of such a central author as Cicero shows that the dividing line between the medieval nucleus and the humanist discoveries may separate the individual works of the same writer. For whereas some of his works, such as the *De inventione* and the *De officiis,* were commonly used during the Middle Ages, his *Brutus,* his letters and many of his orations were rediscovered by the humanists. Less sensational but perhaps more effective was the tremendous activity of the humanists as copyists, and later as editors, of the Latin classics. The wide diffusion and popularity of the Latin classics in the sixteenth century and afterwards would not have been possible without the printing press. In the fourteenth and fifteenth centuries, the introduction of paper as a cheaper writing material and the organization of a regular trade in manuscript books had a similar effect, and the enormous number of manuscript copies of the Latin classics from these centuries has escaped general attention because they have been rarely used by modern editors on account of their late origin. Along with the copying and editing of the Latin authors, the humanists developed the techniques of textual and historical criticism, studied Latin orthography, grammar, and rhetoric, ancient history and mythology, as well as archaeology, epigraphy, and antiquarian subjects. Finally, the humanists produced a vast body of commentaries on the various Latin authors, which are the direct result of their teaching activity and in which they incorporated their philological and historical knowledge as well as their critical judgment. This body of literature is undoubtedly related to the commentaries on Latin authors written by medieval grammarians, but the extent of this connection remains to be investigated, and there is reason to believe that the humanist commentaries became gradually more critical and more scholarly in the course of the Renaissance period.

The humanist study of Greek was much less affected by the tradition of rhetorical practice or by Western medieval precedents. Greek books and Greek instruction were rare exceptions during the Middle Ages;[13] consequently, the work of the humanists appears much more novel when attention is focused on the Greek rather than on the Latin classics. On the other hand, the study of the Greek classics had flourished more or less continually during the medieval centuries in the Byzantine East, and Renaissance humanists in their Greek studies were clearly influenced by scholarly contacts with their Byzantine colleagues. The extent of this influence, not only on the acquisition of particular knowledge but also on the approach and attitude of Western scholars towards Greek literature, cannot yet be estimated at present.[14] As is well known, the humanists introduced Greek into the curric-

ulum of all universities and of the better secondary schools
of Western Europe, and they also imported from the Byzantine and later Turkish East, through purchase and through
less honorable means, a large number of manuscripts con-
taining almost the entire body of extant Greek literature,
which was thus deposited in Western libraries and diffused
through handwritten copies and printed editions. But since
the knowledge of Greek was comparatively rare even during
the Renaissance, whereas Latin remained the common ve-
hicle of learning and instruction, the general diffusion of
Greek literature depended no less on Latin translations than
on editions of the original Greek texts. Thus it was an important, though not yet sufficiently appreciated, achievement
of the Renaissance scholars that they gradually translated
into Latin almost the entire body of Greek literature then
known, and thus introduced it into the main stream of Western thought. Whereas comparatively few writings had been
translated from Greek into Latin in ancient times, during the
later Middle Ages a large body of such translations was
made which covered mainly writings on mathematics, astronomy, and medicine, besides the philosophical works of
Aristotle. The Renaissance humanists supplied many new
versions of the same works which had been translated before, and the relative merits of these competing medieval
and humanist translations have been debated with some pas-
sion, but not yet sufficiently investigated.[15] More obvious
are the merits of the humanists in those numerous cases
where they translated works of Greek antiquity for the first
time. The catalogue of these translations cannot yet be
given in the present state of our knowledge, but it appears
certain that the body of newly translated material includes
practically all of Greek poetry, historiography, and oratory,
much of Greek patristic theology and of non-Aristotelian
philosophy, and even some additional writings on the sciences of mathematics and medicine. The authors all or

most of whose writings thus became known to Western readers include Homer and Sophocles, Herodotus and Thucydides, Xenophon, Isocrates, Demosthenes, Plutarch and Lucian, Epicurus, Sextus and Plotinus, to mention only a few writers of obvious merit or influence. Again, the dividing line between works translated in the Middle Ages and first translated during the Renaissance often separates the individual writings of the same author, as is the case with Plato, Hippocrates, Galen, and Ptolemy, with many Aristotelian commentators and patristic theologians, and even with Aristotle. Thus it will be apparent that both in the Latin and in the Greek fields the Middle Ages possessed a significant selection of classical literature, but that Renaissance humanism extended its knowledge almost to the entire range of its extant remains, that is to the point where modern scholarship has made its further discoveries from palimpsests and papyri.

When we try to assess the contributions of the humanists to the philosophical thought of the Renaissance, we must mention in passing the attempts at a reform of logic, due to Valla, Agricola, Ramus, and Nizolius, which were in part guided by rhetorical considerations, but represent an episode of great historical significance. Yet the most extensive and direct expression of the thought of the humanists proper must be sought in a body of their writings that we have not yet mentioned, namely their treatises and dialogues, many of which deal, as might be expected, with moral questions, including educational, political, and religious problems.[16] Most of these treatises, whether their authors are Petrarch or Salutati, Bruni or Valla, Poggio or Filelfo, Francesco Barbaro or Leone Battista Alberti, are the works of consummate writers and scholars, but must appear somewhat amateurish to a reader acquainted with the works of the greater Greek, scholastic, or modern philosophers. They often seem to lack not only originality, but also coherence, method, and substance, and if we try to sum up their arguments and conclusions, leaving aside citations, examples, and commonplaces, literary ornaments and digressions, we are frequently left with nearly empty hands. Thus I have not been convinced by the attempts to interpret these humanistic treatises as contributions to speculative thought, or to find in humanist philology the seeds of Vico's philosophy of language, although the eighteenth-century philosopher certainly inherited his erudition and his interest in history and literature from the humanists. Nevertheless the humanist treatises are important in many ways and deserve a more thorough study than they have received. They please through the elegance and clarity of their style and their vivid personal and historical flavor as well as through their well-selected and mellowed classical wisdom. They also air or express interesting opinions on matters that occupied the heart and thought of the authors and their contemporaries. They derive added importance from the fact that some of the genuine and more concrete problems of moral philosophy were apparently neglected by the professional philosophers of the time, and thus the humanists prepared the ground for a more systematic treatment of the same problems by later philosophers. This seems to be the function of poets, writers, and amateur thinkers at any time when the professional philosophers are absorbed in technicalities and refuse to discuss certain basic problems.

If we remember the range and extent of humanist scholarship and literature, we shall not be surprised to learn that Isocrates, Plutarch, and Lucian were among their favorite authors, but that the ancient writer who earned their highest admiration was Cicero. Renaissance humanism was an age of Ciceronianism in which the study and imitation of Cicero was a widespread concern, although the exaggeration of this tendency also found its critics. Cicero's influence in the Renaissance has been the subject of more than one study,[17] and we can merely try to state in a few words some of the main features of this influence. Above all, Cicero's rhetorical works provided the theory, and his orations, letters, and dialogues the concrete models for the main branches of prose literature, whereas the structure of his well-cadenced sentences was imitated in all kinds of literary compositions. Through his philosophical writings, he served as a source of information for several schools of Greek philosophy and also as a model of that eclectic type of thinking which was prepared to take its crumbs of knowledge wherever it could find them, and which also characterizes many of the humanist treatises. Finally, the synthesis of philosophy and rhetoric in his work provided the humanists with a favorite ideal, namely the combination of eloquence and wisdom, an ideal which pervades so much of Renaissance literature. It is true that many of the minor humanists were quite satisfied with eloquence alone, or convinced that enough wisdom would come along with it without further effort; whereas many others took shallow commonplaces for wisdom. Yet we should also remember that many of the greater humanists such as Petrarch and Salutati, Valla and Bruni, Alberti and Pontano, Erasmus, More and Montaigne were able to add genuine wisdom to their eloquence.

After the middle of the fifteenth century, the influence of humanistic learning spread outside the limits of the *studia humanitatis* into all areas of Renaissance culture, including philosophy and the various sciences. This was due not only to the fashionable prestige of the humanities, but also to the fact that practically every scholar received a humanistic training in secondary school before he acquired a professional training in any of the other disciplines at the university. On the other hand, some of the humanists also began to realize that a thorough study of philosophy should be added to the *studia humanitatis.*[18] Consequently, we find a number of important thinkers in the fifteenth century, such as Cusanus, Ficino, and Pico, and many more in the sixteenth, who combined a more or less thoroughgoing humanist background with solid philosophical achievements which were derived from different origins.[19] I believe that the discussion of Renaissance humanism in its original meaning has been confused by the attempts to claim these philosophers as an integral part of it, and thus to identify humanism with all or most of Renaissance philosophy. On the other hand, these thinkers should be taken into account if we wish to understand the indirect influence of humanism on Renaissance thought, an influence which in many ways was even more important than its direct contribution.

The pervasive influence of humanism on all aspects of Renaissance culture and especially on its philosophical thought is a vast subject of which we can mention only a few major points. Some influential aspects of Renaissance humanism are characteristic of the age, and not necessarily due to classical influences. There is the emphasis on man, on his dignity and privileged place in the universe, which was forcefully expressed by Petrarch, Manetti, and other humanists, and later elaborated or criticized by many philosophers.[20] This idea was undoubtedly implied in, and connected with, the concept and program of the *studia humanitatis,* and it has provided the opening entry for many modern interpretations of humanism, whenever the specific content of the humanities was left out of account. Another characteristic feature is the tendency to express, and to consider worth expressing, the concrete uniqueness of one's feelings, opinions, experiences, and surroundings, a tendency which appears in the biographical and descriptive literature of the time as well as in its portrait painting, which is present in all the writings of the humanists, and which finds its fullest philosophical expression in Montaigne, who claims that his own self is the main subject matter of his philosophy.[21] This tendency has been adequately described by Burckhardt, who called it "individualism," and those who have debated the individualism of the Renaissance have missed this point entirely when they understand by individualism merely the existence of great individuals, or the nominalist emphasis on the reality of particular things as against universals. Yet more relevant to our purpose are those aspects of humanist influence which are directly connected with its fundamental classicism. I am inclined to find its traces in the taste for elegance, neatness, and clarity of style and literary form which distinguishes the writings of many, if not all, Renaissance scientists and philosophers, and which is not always or entirely a mere external feature. More obvious is the ubiquity of classical sources, quotations, and ideas in Renaissance thought that were either introduced or popularized by the work of the humanists. Without impairing the originality of achievement, this classical element appears in one way or another in all areas, in the visual arts as in the various sciences. Although nearly nothing was known about ancient music, ancient musical theories were used to justify certain innovations of the time, and the humanist reform of handwriting from which our Roman characters are derived was based on the Carolingian minuscule which they mistakenly thought to be the script of the ancient Romans. Livy and Polybius affected the political thought of Machiavelli, Plato that of Thomas More, and Tacitus the theorists of the later sixteenth century. And there was no thinker in the sixteenth century who did not use, besides the traditional texts of Aristotle, Cicero, and Boethius, the newly acquired writings of Plato and the Neoplatonists, of Plutarch and Lucian, of Diogenes Laertius, of Sextus and Epictetus, or the apocryphal works attributed to the Pythagoreans, to Orpheus, Zoroaster, and Hermes Trismegistus.

One more effect of humanism upon Renaissance thought consisted in the repeated attempts to revive or restate the philosophical doctrines of particular ancient thinkers or schools, which in a sense represent the application to philosophy of the revival or renaissance of ancient learning which

was one of the favorite slogans of the humanists, and from
which the much-debated modern name of the period derives
its origin.   Whereas the tendency of most humanists was
rather eclectic, some of them, and also certain other philosophers with a humanist background, preferred a restatement
of some particular ancient doctrine.   Thus we find a kind of
Christianized Epicureanism in Valla; whereas the natural
philosophy of Epicurus found an advocate, after the end of
the Renaissance proper, in Gassendi, and even influenced
some aspects of Galileo's physics.   Stoic philosophy found a
systematic and learned interpreter towards the very end of
the period in Justus Lipsius, whose writings exercised a
strong influence on the moralists of the subsequent centuries.
And various brands of ancient skepticism were adopted, with
some modifications, by Montaigne, Sanchez, and others before they came to influence early modern thought down to
Bayle and Hume.   This tendency also supplies the broader
context for at least some aspects of Renaissance Platonism,
Aristotelianism, and Christianity, as we shall see in the subsequent lectures.

Thus I should like to understand Renaissance humanism,
at least in its origin and in its typical representatives, as a
broad cultural and literary movement, which in its substance
was not philosophical, but had important philosophical im-
plications and consequences.   I have been unable to discover
in the humanist literature any common philosophical doctrine, except a belief in the value of man and the humanities
and in the revival of ancient learning.   Any particular state-
ment gleaned from the work of a humanist may be countered
by contrary assertions in the writings of contemporary authors or even of the same author.   On the other hand, the
common cultural orientation and background might be combined in the case of each author with any set of philosophical
or scientific or theological opinions or cognitions, and actually came to cut across all national, religious, philosophical,

and even professional divisions of the period. ⌈Since the entire range of Greek philosophical and scientific literature was made more completely available to the West than it had been in the Middle Ages or in Roman antiquity, there was a large store of new ideas and notions that had to be tried out and appropriated until its lesson was finally exhausted, and it is this process of intellectual fermentation which characterizes the period and which accounts at least in part for the difference between Thomas Aquinas and Descartes.⌋ For only after this process had been completed, did seventeenth-century philosophy make its new beginning on the basis of early physical science, whereas the heritage of the Renaissance continued to feed many secondary currents of thought down to the nineteenth century.

2. THE ARISTOTELIAN TRADITION

AMONG the many philosophers of classical antiquity, two thinkers have exercised a wider and deeper influence upon posterity than any others, Plato and Aristotle. The controversy and interplay between Platonism and Aristotelianism has occupied a central place in many periods of Western thought, and even the modern student who receives but an elementary introduction to Greek philosophy will inevitably get acquainted with the thought, and with some of the writings, of Plato and of Aristotle. This overwhelming importance of Plato and Aristotle is due to two factors which are in a sense related to each other: the intrinsic greatness of their thought, and the preservation of their writings. Aside from such authors as Sextus Empiricus, Epictetus, Alexander of Aphrodisias, and the Neoplatonists, who represent the latest phases of ancient thought, Plato and Aristotle are the only important Greek philosophers whose writings have been extant, either completely or to a considerable extent. Neither their predecessors such as Heraclitus, Parmenides, or Democritus, nor their successors such as Chrysippus, Panaetius, or Posidonius have been so fortunate, and others such as Theophrastus and Epicurus have fared but slightly better.

Historians of Western thought have often expressed the view that the Renaissance was basically an age of Plato, whereas the Middle Ages had been an age of Aristotle. This view can no longer be maintained without considerable qualifications. In spite of a widespread revolt against the authority of Aristotle, the tradition of Aristotelianism continued to be very strong throughout the Renaissance period, and in some ways it even increased rather than declined. On the other hand, Platonism had its own medieval roots and precedents, and even during the Renaissance, its precise place and the extent of its influence are somewhat elusive and difficult to define, in spite of its undoubted depth and vigor. Nevertheless, Aristotle's influence in the Renaissance was clearly linked with a tradition that originated in the later Middle Ages, and Platonism was understood by its representatives and their contemporaries as a revival. These circumstances may explain why I am going to discuss Aristotle's influence before that of Plato, although Aristotle was Plato's pupil and presupposed the philosophy of his teacher in many ways.

If we want to understand the impact of Aristotle upon later thought, we must remember some curious facts connected with the transmission of his writings.[1] When Aristotle died in 322 B.C., he left a very extensive body of writings which consisted of two completely different groups. On the one hand, there was a large group of dialogues and other popular treatises which had been published during his lifetime, and which continued to be widely read through many centuries until they were finally lost towards the end of antiquity. These popular writings of Aristotle were praised for their literary elegance, and apparently the most famous among them were composed in Aristotle's earlier years and were comparatively close to Plato in their philosophical opinions. The second group of Aristotle's writings, which is the one that has come down to us, represents a collection of the lecture courses which he delivered in his school in Athens. These courses served no literary purpose, but in turn they are highly technical in character, very detailed in their reasoning and in the information supplied, and fairly systematic in their over-all arrangement, forming a vast encyclopaedia of philosophical and scientific knowledge. The systematic writings of Aristotle were not published by him or his immediate successors, but remained for several centuries in the library of his school where they were accessible to its professors, but not to the general public or to the members of other schools of philosophy. Apparently the Aristotelian corpus as we know it was published only between the first century B.C. and the first century A.D., and even some time after that date it does not seem to have been widely read or studied. Until the second century A.D., outside the circle of scholars trained in the Aristotelian school, the systematic writings of Aristotle exercised little or no influence upon the development of ancient thought, and it would be anachronistic to assume such an influence as a major factor in the Platonic Academy, in Stoicism, Epicureanism, or Skepticism, in Philo or in the early Christian thinkers. At the same time, the works and thoughts of Aristotle were transmitted, studied, interpreted, and supplemented by a long series of Aristotelian philosophers in his school, among whom the earliest, Theophrastus, and the last, Alexander of Aphrodisias, are best known to us. Alexander, who lived around 200 A.D., was one of the most authoritative commentators of Aristotle, and also modified the Aristotelian doctrine in a more naturalistic and anti-Platonic direction, denying, for example, the immortality of the soul, a point on which Aristotle had been somewhat ambiguous.

The rise of the Neoplatonic school, which was founded in the third century A.D. and dominated Greek thought down to the end of antiquity in the sixth century, also marks an important phase in the history of Aristotelianism. During that period, Aristotelianism disappeared as a separate school tradition, yet the Neoplatonists themselves were committed to a synthesis of Plato and Aristotle. Consequently, the systematic writings of Aristotle were no less thoroughly studied than the dialogues of Plato; Aristotelian doctrine, especially in logic and natural philosophy, was extensively appropriated, and some of the best and most voluminous commentaries on Aristotle, such as those of Simplicius, are due to members of this school. One Neoplatonic treatise,

Porphyry's introduction to the *Categories,* became almost an integral part of the Aristotelian corpus.

The fact that Aristotle was appropriated and in a sense preserved by the Neoplatonists left profound traces in the later history of Aristotelianism. In trying to follow this history through the Middle Ages, we must distinguish, as for all philosophical and scientific writings of Greek antiquity, three main traditions: the Byzantine, the Arabic, and the Latin.[2] The place of Aristotle in the Byzantine tradition has not yet been, to my knowledge, sufficiently investigated.[3] Yet it is apparent that the writings of the Aristotelian corpus were preserved and transmitted in their original Greek text by Byzantine scholars and copyists, and a number of extant Byzantine commentaries on Aristotle show that the study of his works and thought was by no means neglected. As far as I can make out, the study of Aristotle among the Byzantines was not separated from, or opposed to, the study of Plato and of the ancient Greek poets, or especially connected with theology, except for some very late authors who had been subjected to Western, Latin influences. If I am not mistaken, it was this Byzantine Aristotle, allied with Neoplatonism and literature and an integral part of the classical heritage, whom some of the Greek scholars of the fifteenth century carried along into their Italian exile and who exercised some influence upon the Aristotelian studies of the later Renaissance.

Very different, and for its impact upon the Western Middle Ages, more important, was the history of Aristotle among the Arabs.[4] When the Arabs began to translate the works of Greek literature that interested them, they largely omitted the Greek poets, orators, and historians, and centered their efforts on the most authoritative writers in such fields as mathematics and astronomy, medicine, astrology and alchemy, and philosophy. The translated Greek works provided the nucleus of subject matter in these disciplines, to which the Arabs subsequently added their own contributions. As far as philosophy is concerned, the Arabs acquired an almost complete corpus of Aristotle's systematic writings, along with some Neoplatonic and other commentaries on them, and with a certain number of Neoplatonic treatises. Thus the Arabs inherited Aristotle from the Neoplatonic tradition of late antiquity, and consequently, their understanding of Aristotle was affected by Neoplatonic interpretations and accretions which they were never able to eliminate completely. On the other hand, Aristotle attained among the Arabs an authority and doctrinal preponderance that he had never possessed in Greek antiquity to the very end. Apparently the Arabs did not acquire the complete writings of Plato and of the major Neoplatonists, and thus the sheer bulk of Aristotle's writings, along with their commentaries and with the apocrypha, outweighed all other Greek philosophical literature available to them. Moreover, these writings imposed themselves by the solidity of their content, and by the systematic and encyclopaedic character of the corpus, which lent itself to painstaking study and which comprised, besides such disciplines as logic, rhetoric, poetics, ethics, and metaphysics, also a number of others which have since been detached from philosophy as separate sciences, such as economics and psychology, physics and natural history. The Aristotelian corpus, supplemented by medicine and mathematics, seemed to represent a complete encyclopaedia of learning whose various writings coincided with the branches of knowledge as such. The authority of Aristotle was probably further enhanced by that of Galen, who was strongly influenced by Aristotelian philosophy and exercised a similar influence upon Arabic medicine, especially since some of the most important Arabic thinkers combined philosophy and medicine in their work. Thus the major Arabic philosophers, such as Avicenna and Averroes, were commentators and followers of Aristotle, and Averroes even tended to reduce the Neoplatonic additions and to attain a purer understanding of Aristotle. As is well known, the Aristotelianism of the Arabs, and especially that of Averroes, exercised a powerful influence upon the Jewish thought of the later Middle Ages, when Maimonides was the leading representative of Aristotelianism, and strongly affected the philosophy of the Christian West even after its tradition had come to a sudden end in the Islamic world itself, as a result of new religious and political developments.

If we want to understand the history of thought and learning in the Western Latin Middle Ages, we must first of all realize that it had its foundation in Roman, and not in Greek antiquity. The Romans produced, under the impact of Greek models, a distinguished literature in poetry and in prose; they appropriated the grammatical and rhetorical learning of the Greeks, and they made a lasting original contribution in the field of jurisprudence, but they did not develop a significant philosophical tradition. Rome and the other Western centers had flourishing schools of rhetoric, but no schools of philosophy comparable to those of Athens and Alexandria. The efforts to develop a technical vocabulary for philosophical discourse in the Latin language remained in the beginning stages until the end of antiquity. Few outstanding works of Greek philosophers were translated into Latin, and the philosophical literature produced by the Romans was mostly of a popularizing nature. Among the Greek sources of this literature Aristotle occupies a very minor place, compared with the Platonists, Stoics, Skeptics or Epicureans. He appears to be unknown to, or to have no importance for, Lucretius, Seneca, or St. Augustine; and even Cicero is chiefly acquainted with the published works of Aristotle that are now lost, and barely mentions the systematic writings which dominated the later tradition. The one significant exception is represented by one of the latest writers of Roman antiquity, Boethius, who translated two of Aristotle's logical works, the *Categories* and the treatise *On Interpretation,* along with Porphyry's introduction.

During the early Middle Ages, the Latin West was largely cut off from the richer Greek tradition and reduced to the indigenous resources of Roman literature, which was weak in philosophy, as we have noticed. The body of secular learning provided in the monastic and cathedral schools of the period was limited to the elementary encyclopaedia of the seven liberal arts, that is, grammar, rhetoric, dialectic, arithmetic, geometry, astronomy, and music. In this scheme, which prevailed to the eleventh century, grammar was the leading subject, which included at times the study of the Latin poets. Philosophy was represented only by dialectic, that is, elementary logic, and this subject was largely based on the Aristotelian treatises translated by Boethius. Philosophy in the broad sense of the word as known to the ancient Greeks was almost forgotten, and the only author who made a genuine contribution to philosophical thought in that period, Scotus Eriugena, was an isolated figure distinguished for his acquaintance with Greek Neoplatonism.

This situation was completely changed through the remarkable rise of philosophical, theological, and scientific studies that began during the second half of the eleventh century and culminated in the thirteenth. During that period, the body of learning expanded steadily until it surpassed the traditional limits of the seven arts. A large amount of writings on philosophy, on the sciences and the pseudo sciences was translated from Arabic and from Greek that introduced precious material previously unavailable in Latin and tended to stimulate and transform Western thought.[5] Among the philosophical authors thus translated, Proclus and other Neoplatonic authors were well represented, but the most extensive and most important body of literature consisted of the nearly complete corpus of Aristotle, accompanied by a few Greek commentaries, and by a much larger body of Arabic commentaries, especially by Avicenna and Averroes. The writings of Aristotle and of his Greek commentators as well as of Proclus were in part translated from the original text, to be sure, but the selection of subjects and of authors clearly reflects the Arabic rather than the ancient Greek tradition of philosophy. At the same time, new institutions of higher learning developed, the universities, which differed considerably from the earlier schools in their curriculum, textbooks, and methods of instruction.[6] The instruction centered around the *lectura,* the continuous reading and exposition of a standard text, and the *disputatio,* the public discussion of a proposed thesis with the help of formalized arguments. These forms of instruction produced the two main types of medieval scholarly literature, the commentary and the question. The subject matter of university instruction was fixed during the thirteenth century at Paris and the other Northern universities in the system of four faculties, theology, law, medicine, and arts or philosophy. Whereas the teaching of theology was based on the Bible and on Peter Lombard's *Sentences,* and that of law on the Corpus Juris of Justinian and on Gratian's *Decretum,* the instruction in medicine and in philosophy came to be based on some of the new translations from the Greek and Arabic. The philosophical disciplines thus became for the first time in the Latin world subjects of separate instruction, and the texts adopted for this instruction, after some resistance, were the writings of Aristotle along with those of Averroes and of other commentators. The chief subjects were logic and natural philosophy, whereas ethics and metaphysics attained the status of elective courses only. Thus the writings of Aristotle had become by the middle of the thirteenth century the basis of philosophical instruction at the universities. They owed this position not merely to Arabic precedent, but also to the solidity of their content and to their systematic and encyclopaedic character. Aristotle was not studied as a "great book," but as a textbook that was the starting point for commentaries and questions and supplied a frame of reference for all trained philosophical thinkers even when they ventured to reinterpret him, or to depart from his doctrine, according to their own opinions. The Aristotelianism of the later Middle Ages was characterized not so much by a common system of ideas as by a common source material, a common terminology, a common set of definitions and problems, and a common method of discussing these problems. There was offered a variety of interpretations for many passages in Aristotle, and of solutions for the most debated problems, some of which grew out of medieval philosophical preoccupations rather than from Aristotle's own writings. The understanding of this vast and complex philosophical literature has made much progress in recent years, yet it is still hampered by the failure to distinguish clearly between philosophy and theology, which were separate disciplines, by an excessive faith in such general labels as Thomism, Scotism, Occamism, and Averroism, and by a tendency to focus attention too exclusively on St. Thomas Aquinas and his school. The Aristotelian philosophers of the thirteenth and fourteenth centuries were engaged in the discussion of numerous detailed problems, especially in logic and physics, and offered a great variety of solutions for each of them. Whereas it might be possible to group them roughly according to the stand taken on a particular issue, they may show a very different alignment with reference to some other issue.[7] Thomas Aquinas went farthest among his contemporaries in his attempt to reconcile Aristotelian philosophy and Christian theology, and his writings are distinguished by their clarity and coherence. Yet in his own time, he enjoyed no monopoly of authority or of orthodoxy; his teachings were in competition with many others, and sometimes even condemned, and much of his work belongs, by medieval standards, to theology rather than to philosophy.

His authority was soon established within his own Domini-can order, but outside that order, the doctrines of Duns Scotus and of William of Ockham were much more influen-tial, and the important developments in logic and physics which took place during the fourteenth century at Oxford and Paris were largely due to the Occamist school. Most ambiguous and controversial of all is the term Averroism which has been applied by historians to one particular trend of medieval Aristotelianism.[8] If we understand by Aver-roism the use of Averroes' commentary on Aristotle, every medieval Aristotelian including Aquinas was an Averroist. If we limit the term to all those thinkers who made a neat distinction between reason and faith, Aristotelian philosophy and Christian theology, practically all teachers of philoso-phy, as distinct from the theologians, took that position, from the later thirteenth century through the fourteenth and later. Finally, if we mean by Averroism the adherence to one dis-tinctive doctrine of Averroes, namely the unity of the intel-lect in all men, we are singling out a much smaller group of thinkers who still differ among each other on the numerous other questions which occupied and divided the Aristotelian philosophers of the period. Hence it will be best to use these labels with great caution, and to emphasize the fact that the Aristotelian tradition of the later Middle Ages com-prised a great variety of thinkers and of ideas held together by the common reference to the corpus of Aristotle's writ-ings, which constituted the basic material of reading and dis-cussion in the philosophical disciplines.

I seem to have given an undue share of my allotted time today to a discussion of medieval rather than Renaissance developments. Yet it has been my intention to show how Aristotle had become by the early fourteenth century "the master of those who know," in order to emphasize the addi-tional fact, which is less widely known, that this Aristotelian tradition, though exposed to attacks and subject to transformations, continued strongly and vigorously to the end of the sixteenth century and even later. The failure to appreciate this fact is due to various reasons. Historians, like journalists, are apt to concentrate on news and to forget that there is a complex and broad situation which remained unaffected by the events of the moment. They also have for some time been more interested in the origins rather than in the continuations of intellectual and other developments. More specifically, many historians of thought have been sympathetic to the opponents of Aristotelianism in the Renaissance, whereas most of the defenders of medieval philosophy have limited their efforts to its earlier phases before the end of the thirteenth century, and have sacrificed the late scholastics to the critique of their contemporary and modern adversaries. Yet we have learned through recent studies that the chief progress made during the later fourteenth century in the fields of logic and natural philosophy was due to the Aristotelian, and more specifically, to the Occamist school at Paris and Oxford. During the fifteenth and sixteenth centuries, university instruction in the philosophical disciplines continued everywhere to be based on the works of Aristotle; consequently, most professional teachers of philosophy followed the Aristotelian tradition, used its terminology and method, discussed its problems, and composed commentaries and questions on Aristotle. Only a few individual thinkers and schools have been studied so far, and the large extent of this tradition, and of its proportional share in the philosophical literature of the Renaissance period, is not generally realized. This Aristotelian orientation of the university philosophers can be traced at Paris,⁹ Louvain, and other centers far into the sixteenth century, although it has not been studied very much. It disappears from sight at Oxford and Cambridge after the end of the fourteenth century, but there is reason to believe that this is due to lack of scholarly attention rather than lack of facts or source materials. It flourished, in close alliance with Catholic theology, well into the seventeenth century at Salamanca, Alcalà, and Coimbra, and the influence of this Spanish neoscholasticism extended, through its most famous representative, Franciscus Suarez, well beyond the borders of the Iberian peninsula or of Catholicism.[10] Also at the German universities, Aristotelianism was strong and productive through the fifteenth century, and continued to flourish long after the Protestant Reformation, for in spite of Luther's dislike for scholasticism, and thanks to the influence of Melanchthon, Aristotle remained the chief source of academic instruction in the philosophical disciplines.[11] Thus it is not surprising if even later philosophers who turned far away from scholasticism, such as Bacon, Descartes, Spinoza, or Leibniz, still show in their terminology, in their arguments, and in some of their doctrines the traces of that tradition which was still alive in the schools and universities of their time, although we should realize that these thinkers absorbed at the same time also different influences which we might roughly describe as humanistic, Platonist, Stoic, or skeptical.[12]

We have not yet spoken about the place of Aristotelianism in Italy, a country which differed from the rest of Europe in many respects even during the Middle Ages and which occupied such an important position during the Renaissance period. The customary views on the Italian Renaissance might easily lead us to believe that Aristotelian scholasticism flourished in medieval Italy as in the North, but was abandoned in Italy sooner than elsewhere under the impact of Renaissance humanism. The actual facts suggest almost exactly the opposite. Up to the last decades of the thirteenth century, instruction at the Italian universities was almost entirely limited to formal rhetoric, law, and medicine. Scholastic theology was largely confined to the schools of the mendicant orders; and those famous scholastic theologians and philosophers who happened to be Italian, such as Lanfranc,

Anselm and Peter Lombard, St. Bonaventura and St. Thomas Aquinas, did most of their studying and teaching at Paris and other Northern centers. After some earlier appearance at Salerno and Naples, Aristotelian philosophy became for the first time firmly established at Bologna and other Italian universities towards the very end of the thirteenth century,[13] that is, at the same time that the first signs of a study of the Latin classics began to announce the coming rise of Italian humanism. Simultaneously with humanism, Italian Aristotelianism developed steadily through the fourteenth century under the influence of Paris and Oxford, became more independent and more productive through the fifteenth century,[14] and attained its greatest development during the sixteenth and early seventeenth centuries, in such comparatively well known thinkers as Pomponazzi, Zabarella, and Cremonini. In other words, as far as Italy is concerned, Aristotelian scholasticism, just like classical humanism, is fundamentally a phenomenon of the Renaissance period whose ultimate roots can be traced in a continuous development to the very latest phase of the Middle Ages. The greatest difference between this Italian Aristotelianism and its Northern counterpart, aside from the times of their respective rise and decline, is related to the organization of the universities and their faculties or schools. In Paris and the other Northern centers, philosophy was taught in the faculty of arts, which also included what was left of the seven liberal arts, and which served as preparation for the three higher faculties of law, medicine, and theology, and especially for the latter. At Bologna and the other Italian centers, there were only two faculties, that of law and that of the arts. There never was a separate faculty of theology. Within the faculty of arts, medicine was the most important subject of instruction, logic and natural philosophy were considered as preparatory for medicine and occupied the second place, whereas grammar, rhetoric, and moral philosophy, mathematics and astronomy, theology and metaphysics came last. As in the North, logic and natural philosophy were considered the most important philosophical disciplines and taught on the basis of Aristotle and his commentators, but this instruction was and always remained linked with medicine and unrelated to theology.

Under the misleading name of "Paduan Averroism," some phases of this Italian Aristotelianism have been studied during the last hundred years or so, but much of the literature produced by it remains unpublished or unread. It consists in commentaries and questions on the works of Aristotle, and in independent treatises on related problems. The labels used for it such as Thomism, Scotism and Occamism, Averroism and Alexandrism are, as usual, inadequate. Their work consists, like that of their Northern predecessors and contemporaries, in a detailed discussion of many minute questions where each particular issue was likely to produce a variety of solutions and a different alignment of individual thinkers. Again they agree in their method and terminology, and in their constant reference to Aristotle and his commentators, but there are few philosophical doctrines common to all of them. The separation between philosophy and theology, reason or Aristotle and faith or religious authority, was consistently maintained, without leading to a direct conflict or opposition. Besides rational argument, sense perception or experience was emphasized as the major or only source of natural knowledge, and this might justify us in speaking of a kind of empiricism. In the sixteenth century, Averroes' doctrine of the unity of the intellect for all men continued to be discussed, although it was accepted only by some of the Aristotelian philosophers. At the same time, the related problem of immortality became the center of discussion through a famous and controversial treatise of Pomponazzi, who rejected the unity of the intellect but maintained that the immortality of the soul cannot be demonstrated on ra-

tional or Aristotelian principles. Later Aristotelians such
as Zabarella participated in the discussion on the nature of
the cognitive method, and formulated the doctrine that
natural knowledge proceeds through analysis from the ob-
served phenomena to their inferred causes, and returns
through synthesis from the latter to the former, a doctrine
that was at least partly rooted in the Aristotelian tradition
and influenced in turn so anti-Aristotelian a scientist as
Galileo.[15] Among the Aristotelian philosophers of the Italian Renaissance, the strongest influences were apparently
those of Occamism and of the so-called Averroism, which
were gradually modified by various contemporary developments. At the same time, Thomism and Scotism continued
to flourish among the theologians. Scotism seems to have
been the more active and more widely diffused current, but
the Italian Renaissance produced such authoritative Thom-
ists as Caietanus, and the Dominican teaching affected many
other theologians, and also such non-Thomist philosophers
as Ficino and Pomponazzi. If we add to this the authority
attached to Thomas by the Jesuits and by the Council of
Trent, and the increasing use of his *Summa,* instead of Peter
Lombard's *Sentences,* as a textbook of theology,[16] we may
very well say that the sixteenth century marks a notable ad-
vance over the thirteenth and fourteenth centuries in the rela-
ive role and importance of Thomism, and a conspicuous step
towards that adoption of Thomism as the official philosophy
of the Catholic Church which was finally codified in 1879.

After this all-too-brief discussion of Renaissance Aristotelianism in its close relations to the later Middle Ages, I
should like to mention those changes and modifications
which it underwent under the impact of the new attitudes
of the period, and especially of classical humanism. The
keynote of this change was sounded by Petrarch when he
suggested that Aristotle was better than his translators and
commentators, and the general tendency was to take Aris-

totle out of his isolation as a textbook authority into the company of the other ancient philosophers and writers.[17] Western scholars learned from their Byzantine teachers to study the works of Aristotle in the Greek original. Humanist professors began to lecture on Aristotle as one of the classical Greek authors, and Aristotelian philosophers who had enjoyed a humanist education were led to refer to the original text of their chief authority. Although practically the whole corpus of Aristotle's works had been translated into Latin during the later Middle Ages, the Renaissance humanists used their increased knowledge of the Greek language and literature to supply new Latin versions of Aristotle which competed with their medieval predecessors and gradually penetrated into the university curriculum. The merits of these humanist translations in relation to the medieval ones have been debated ever since their own time, and obviously vary according to the abilities of the individual translators. They show a better knowledge of syntax, idioms, and textual variants, and also a greater freedom in word order, style, and terminology. The changes in terminology were a serious matter in an author who served as a standard text in philosophy, and the net result was to present an Aristotle who was different from that of the medieval tradition. Moreover, there were a few additions made to the Aristotelian corpus, and some of the writings previously available acquired a novel importance or a novel place in the system of learning. The *Eudemian Ethics* was translated for the first time, and so were the *Mechanics* and some other writings of the early Aristotelian school. The *Theology* of Aristotle, an apocryphal work of Arabic origin and Neoplatonic tendency, was used to emphasize the agreement between Plato and Aristotle, and the fragments of Aristotle's lost early writings were collected for the same purpose.[18] The humanists who considered moral philosophy as a part of their domain and often held the chair of ethics continued to use the *Nicomachean Ethics* and *Politics* as their main texts, and thus were led to give to Aristotle's doctrine an important share in their eclectic views on moral, educational, and political questions. Aristotle's *Rhetoric,* which in the Middle Ages had been neglected by the professional rhetoricians and treated by the scholastic philosophers as an appendix to the *Ethics* and *Politics,*[19] became during the sixteenth century an important text for the humanist rhetoricians. The *Poetics,* not completely unknown to the Latin Middle Ages,[20] as scholars had long believed, but still comparatively neglected, attained through the humanists a wide circulation and became in the sixteenth century the standard text which gave rise to a large body of critical discussion and literature;[21] and it is curious to note that the authority of Aristotle's *Poetics* attained its climax in the same seventeenth century which witnessed the overthrow of his *Physics.* Finally, if we pass from the humanist scholars to the professional philosophers and scientists, it appears that the most advanced work of Aristotle's logic, the *Posterior Analytics,* received greater attention in the sixteenth century than before, and that at the same time an increased study of Aristotle's biological writings accompanied the contemporary progress in botany, zoology, and natural history.[22]

With reference to those works of Aristotle which were and remained the center of instruction in logic and natural philosophy, the most important changes derived from the fact that the works of the ancient Greek commentators became completely available in Latin between the late fifteenth and the end of the sixteenth centuries, and were more and more used to balance the interpretations of the medieval Arabic and Latin commentators. The Middle Ages had known their works only in a very limited selection or through quotations in Averroes. Ermolao Barbaro's translation of Themistius and Girolamo Donato's version of Alexander's *De anima* were among the most important ones in a long line of others. When modern historians speak of Alexandrism as a current within Renaissance Aristotelianism that was opposed to Averroism, they are justified in part by the fact that the Greek commentators, that is, Alexander and also Themistius, Simplicius, and many others, were increasingly drawn upon for the exposition of Aristotle. In a more particular sense, Alexander's specific notion that the human soul was mortal received more attention from the Aristotelian philosophers. Thus the change and increase in Aristotelian source material led in many instances to a doctrinal change in the interpretation of the philosopher or in the philosophical position defended in the name of reason, nature, and Aristotle, and these doctrinal changes were further enhanced under the impact of both classical and contemporary ideas of different, non-Aristotelian origin. Thus Pomponazzi, who is rightly considered an outstanding representative of the Aristotelian school, emphasizes such non-Aristotelian doctrines as the central position of man in the universe and the importance of the practical rather than the speculative intellect for human happiness, which are both of humanistic origin; defends the Stoic doctrine of fate against Alexander of Aphrodisias; and follows Plato and the Stoics in stressing that moral Such amalgamations of diverse doctrines are bound to oc- virtue is its own reward, vice its own greatest punishment.[23] cur in any genuine philosophical tradition dedicated to the pursuit of truth rather than of orthodoxy, and they become harmful only when they are used to distort the historical facts or to bolster the dogmatic claims of a particular tradition. The gradual nature of the change which affected Renaissance Aristotelianism and which I have been trying to describe is apparent when we compare the works of two outstanding Aristotelian philosophers of the early and of the late sixteenth century. Jacopo Zabarella, who represents the later phase, had acquired a full command of the Greek Aristotle and of his ancient commentators, and thus he has been praised by modern scholars not only as a good philosopher, but also as one of the best and most lucid Aristotelian commentators of all ages. Pietro Pomponazzi, who died in 1525, knew no Greek and was still deeply imbued with the traditions of medieval Aristotelianism, but he eagerly seized upon the new source material made available by his humanist contemporaries, and derived from Alexander the idea that the immortality of the human soul could not be demonstrated on rational or Aristotelian principles. Thus the classical scholarship of the humanists, applied to Aristotle and to his Greek commentators, had an indirect but powerful effect upon the continuing tradition of philosophical Aristotelianism through the sixteenth century and afterwards.

Our picture of the Renaissance attitude towards Aristotle would be incomplete if we failed to discuss the strong currents of anti-Aristotelianism which have been often exaggerated or misunderstood but which do occupy an important place in Renaissance thought. The rebellion against the authority of Aristotle or at least against his medieval interpreters is indeed a recurrent feature in the writings of many Renaissance thinkers from Petrarch to Bruno and Galileo. When we examine this polemic in each case for its reasons, content, and results, instead of taking its charges and claims at their face value, we are led to the conclusion that the anti-Aristotelianism of the Renaissance laid the ground for certain later developments, to be sure, but that it was in its own time neither unified nor effective. When we listen to Petrarch's attacks against Aristotle and his medieval followers, we are apt to forget that the Aristotelianism which he attacked had been established at the universities for hardly a hundred years, and in Italy even more recently. Thus a younger generation tends to believe that it is overthrowing a tradition of many centuries when in fact this tradition had been barely established by its fathers or grandfathers. The humanist attacks against scholasticism from which Aristotle himself was often exempted are known from several documents of the fifteenth century, from Leonardo Bruni to Ermolao Barbaro.[24] This polemic turned out to be ineffective inasmuch as the humanists criticized the bad style of their opponents, their ignorance of classical sources, and their preoccupation with supposedly unimportant questions, but failed to make positive contributions to the philosophical and scientific disciplines with which the scholastics were concerned. If we keep in mind the cultural and professional divisions of the period, and the flourishing state of Aristotelian philosophy in Renaissance Italy, we are inclined to view this polemic in its proper perspective, that is, as an understandable expression of departmental rivalry, and as a phase in the everlasting battle of the arts of which many other examples may be cited from ancient, medieval, or modern times.[25] Only in some instances did Renaissance humanists succeed in attacking their scholastic opponents on their own ground. There was a persistent tendency which began with Valla and culminated in Ramus and Nizolius to reform Aristotelian logic with the help of rhetoric, and during the latter part of the sixteenth century as well as much of the seventeenth, Ramism was a serious rival of Aristotelian logic in the schools of Germany, Great Britain, and America.[26] On the other hand, the Spanish humanist Vives made the ambitious attempt to substitute a classical and humanist encyclopaedia of learning for the medieval one and exercised a deep and wide influence on Western education.[27]

Renaissance Platonism, which many historians have been inclined to oppose to medieval Aristotelianism, was not as persistently anti-Aristotelian as we might expect. Its most influential representatives were either impressed by the

Neoplatonic synthesis of Plato and Aristotle, or even directly affected by medieval Aristotelianism. Thus Marsilio Ficino would follow Plato in metaphysics, but Aristotle in natural philosophy, a view which is reflected in Raphael's School of Athens, and Pico della Mirandola expressly defended the medieval Aristotelians against the humanist attacks of Ermolao Barbaro.[28]

It was only during the sixteenth century that Aristotelianism began to be attacked in its central territory, that is, in natural philosophy. A series of brilliant thinkers, not unaffected by Aristotelianism or other traditions, but original in their basic intention, people like Paracelsus, Telesio, Patrizi, Bruno, and others,[29] began to propose rival systems of cosmology and of natural philosophy which made an impression upon their contemporaries and have been of lasting interest to historians of Renaissance thought. They failed to overthrow the Aristotelian tradition in natural philosophy, not because they were persecuted, or because their opponents preferred vested interests and habits of thought to the truth, but because their impressive doctrines were not based on a firm and acceptable method. Aristotelian natural philosophy, rich in subject matter and solid in concepts, could not possibly be displaced from the university curriculum as long as there was no comparable body of teachable doctrine that could have taken its place. This was not supplied by the humanists, the Platonists, or the natural philosophers of the later Renaissance, who could dent but not break the Aristotelian tradition. The decisive attack upon the natural philosophy of the Aristotelians came from Galileo and the other physicists of the seventeenth century.

This momentous event in the history of modern thought has often been represented rather crudely as a victory of "Science" and the "Scientific Method" over superstition or a mistaken tradition. There is no such thing as Science or the Scientific Method, but there is a complex body of various sciences and other forms of knowledge whose unity remains an ideal program, and there are various methods of attaining valid knowledge and of judging its validity. In the period preceding Galileo with which we are concerned, the various sciences differed in their traditions and mutual relations. Mathematics and astronomy were largely separate from philosophy and the Aristotelian tradition, and made notable advances during the sixteenth century without affecting that tradition in a serious way.[30] Medicine was another science distinct from philosophy, but more closely linked to it since medicine and philosophy were considered as parts of the same study and career, and since such medical authorities as Galen and Avicenna were Aristotelians. Nevertheless, notable progress was made in such medical disciplines as anatomy and surgery, that were based on observation and comparatively removed from the philosophical and medical theories of the time. On the other hand, natural philosophy as then understood and taught from the works of Aristotle, comprised such sciences as physics and biology. Even the development of these two sciences took a different course with reference to Aristotelianism. In biology, great progress was made during the sixteenth century and even afterwards within the framework of the Aristotelian tradition. In physics, on the other hand, the very conception of Aristotelian physics had to be overthrown in order to make room for modern physics. The Aristotelian physics of the later Middle Ages and of the Renaissance was not as wrong or absurd as older scholars had assumed, nor was Galileo as unaffected by it as he himself or some of his modern admirers believed.[31] Yet for the Aristotelians, physics was a matter of qualities, not of quantities, and its objects on earth were essentially different from the stars in heaven. Consequently, Aristotelian physics was closely linked with formal logic, but separated from mathematics and even to some extent from astronomy.

Galileo, the professional mathematician and astronomer who claimed to be a natural philosopher, postulated a new physics based on experiments and calculations, a physics of quantities that had for its foundation not formal logic, but mathematics, and that was to be closely related to astronomy.[32] Once this new physics had been firmly established in its methods and had begun to yield more and more specific results, it was bound to undermine the prestige of traditional Aristotelian physics and eventually to drive it from its place in the curriculum. This happened during the seventeenth and early eighteenth centuries, and it could not possibly have happened in the sixteenth. Our impatient enthusiasm for the achievements of a later period should not prompt us to read them back into an earlier epoch, or to blame the latter for not having anticipated them. To be sure, individual thinkers are always capable of startling insights, but a large group of people is likely to change its modes of thought rather slowly unless it is suddenly shaken by fashion, by violent experiences, or by political compulsion.

Thus we may conclude that the authority of Aristotle was challenged during the Renaissance in different ways and for different reasons, but that it remained quite strong, especially in the field of natural philosophy. This was due not so much to professional inertia as to the wealth and solidity of subject matter contained in the Aristotelian writings, to which its critics for some time could not oppose anything comparable. The concepts and methods that were bound to overthrow Aristotelian physics were just being discussed and prepared during the sixteenth century, but did not bear visible and lasting fruits before the seventeenth. The anti-Aristotelian revolution which marks the beginning of the modern period in the physical sciences and in philosophy had some of its roots and forerunners in the Renaissance period, but did not actually occur until later.

The Renaissance is still in many respects an Aristotelian age which in part continued the trends of medieval Aristotelianism, and in part gave it a new direction under the influence of classical humanism and other different ideas.

3. RENAISSANCE PLATONISM

PLATO'S influence on Western thought has been so broad and profound, and in spite of occasional voices of dissent, so continuous, that a great contemporary thinker has been able to state that the history of Western philosophy may be characterized as a series of footnotes to Plato.[1] Yet if we examine the actual ideas of those thinkers who have professed their indebtedness to the Athenian philosopher or who have been called Platonists by themselves or by others, we do not only find, as might be expected, a series of different interpretations and reinterpretations of Plato's teachings and writings. We are also confronted with the puzzling fact that different Platonists have selected, emphasized, and developed different doctrines or passages from Plato's works. Hardly a single notion which we associate with Plato has been held by all Platonists, neither the transcendent existence of universal forms nor the direct knowledge of these intelligible entities, neither spiritual love nor the immortality of the soul, let alone his outline of the perfect state. Thus it is possible for two thinkers who have been conventionally and perhaps legitimately classified as Platonists to have very different philosophies, or even to have not a single specific doctrine in common. The term Platonism does not lend itself very well as a middle term to the arithmetic or syllogistics of sources and influences, unless the specific texts and notions involved in each case are spelled out in all their detail. Moreover, ever since classical antiquity, Platonist philosophers have tried not so much to repeat or restate Plato's doctrines in their original form, as to combine them with notions of diverse origin, and these accretions, like the tributaries of a broadening river, became integral parts of the continuing tradition. They are as necessary for a proper understanding of the history of Platonism, as they might be misleading if used uncritically for an interpretation of Plato himself. It is only during the last 150 years or so that modern scholarship has attempted to cleanse the genuine thought of Plato from the mire of the Platonic tradition. This effort has yielded in part very solid results, yet today we are beginning to feel that there has been a tendency to exaggerate the differences between Plato and later Platonism, and to overlook certain genuine features in Plato's thought that may be alien to modern science and philosophy, but served as a starting point for his earlier interpreters.[2] Thus an archaeologist who tries to remove the crust of later centuries from a Greek statue must be careful not to damage its incomparably subtle surface.

This complex and even elusive nature of the Platonic tradition is partly due to the character of Plato's thought and writings. Among all major Greek philosophers until Plotinus, Plato had the unique fortune of having his works, as far as we can tell, completely preserved. These works are literary compositions written and published in different periods of a long and eventful life. They are in the form of dialogues which sometimes end without apparent conclusion and in which different views are proposed and discussed by different persons. Since Plato rarely speaks in his own name, it seems difficult to identify his own definite opinions, or to separate them from those of Socrates, Parmenides, and his other characters. Moreover, some of the most coherent passages are presented in the ambiguous form of myths, similes, or digressions. Finally, the different dialogues, though not completely unrelated in their subject matter, fail to suggest any order or connection that might lead to a philosophical system. Modern scholarship has tried to overcome these difficulties through the historical method, to establish a chronological sequence for the authentic dialogues, and to supplement their content with the statements of Aristotle and others about Plato's oral teaching. This historical approach was foreign to the Platonist scholars of classical antiquity. They merely collected all works attributed to Plato in a single edition, thus giving them the appearance of a systematic order which to us seems artificial. In this manner, a number of apocryphal pieces found their way into the Platonic corpus and continued to influence the subsequent tradition, although the authenticity of certain Platonic works was already questioned in antiquity.

Plato's influence upon later Greek thought was dependent not only on his dialogues which were generally available to the reading public, but also on the school which he founded and which continued as an institution for many centuries until 529 A.D. Since Plato left no systematic writings to his school, and since even his oral teaching was apparently not of a dogmatic character, the philosophical tradition in his Academy was subject to much greater changes and fluctuations than in the other philosophical schools of antiquity. Plato's immediate successors in the Academy modified his doctrine as we know it hardly less than did another pupil, Aristotle,[3] and during the third century B.C. the Academy turned towards a more or less radical skepticism to which it clung for more than two hundred years. In the meantime, Plato's dialogues were read and admired outside his school, and strongly affected the thought of such Stoic philosophers as Panaetius and Posidonius. Around the beginning of our era, a popular and somewhat eclectic kind of Platonism that borrowed various elements from Aristotle and especially from Stoicism had replaced Skepticism in the Athenian Academy, had established a kind of school in Alexandria and perhaps in other centers, and had begun to pervade the thought of a widening circle of philosophical and popular writers.[4] This movement, which is now commonly called Middle Platonism, made at least one important contribution to the history of Platonism, for it formulated the doctrine, ever since attributed to Plato but hardly found in his dialogues, that the transcendent ideas or intelligible forms are concepts of a divine intelligence. Middle Platonism had many elements in common with the Neopythagoreanism which flourished during the first centuries of our era and forged many Platonizing works under the name of Pythagoras and his early pupils, and with the Hermetics, a circle of pagan theologians who flourished in Alexandria and composed a corpus of writings that were attributed to the Egyptian divinity Hermes Trismegistus.[5] When Philo the Jew, and after him the Alexandrian Church Fathers Clement and Origen, made the first attempts to combine the teachings of Biblical religion with Greek philosophy, it was the Platonism popular at their time which supplied the most numerous and most important doctrinal elements. Thus the ground was well prepared both among pagans and Christians when philosophical Platonism was revived during the third century A.D. in Alexandria by Ammonius Saccas and by his great pupil, Plotinus.

This school, which called itself Platonic and which modern historians have named Neoplatonic to emphasize its differences from Plato, chose Plato's dialogues for its chief philosophical authority, but tried to fit Plato's scattered doctrines into a coherent system and to incorporate in it other ideas derived from the Stoics and especially from Aristotle. As a comprehensive synthesis of Greek thought, Neoplatonism thus dominated the latest phase of ancient philosophy and bequeathed its heritage to subsequent ages. Beneath the surface of the common school tradition, there are many significant differences of doctrine that have not yet been fully explored. To the genuine elements derived from Plato, Plotinus added a more explicit emphasis on a

hierarchical universe that descends through several levels
from the transcendent God or One to the corporeal world,
and on an inner, spiritual experience that enables the self
to reascend through the intelligible world to that supreme
One; whereas the physical world is conceived, probably under the influence of Posidonius, as a web of hidden affinities
originating in a world soul and other cosmic souls. In
Proclus, one of the last heads of the Athenian school, Neoplatonism attains its most systematic and even schematic
perfection. In his *Elements of Theology* and *Platonic Theology* all things and their mutual relations are neatly defined
and deduced in their proper place and order; and the concepts of Aristotle's logic and metaphysics, divested of their
specific and concrete reference, are used as elements of a
highly abstract and comprehensive ontology.[6] As a commentator, Proclus applied this neat and scholastic system
to some of Plato's dialogues, just as other members of the
school applied it to Aristotle. And as the leading philosophy of the period, Neoplatonism supplied practically all
later Greek Church Fathers and theologians with their
philosophical terms and concepts, most of all that obscure
father of most Christian mysticism who hides under the
name of Dionysius the Areopagite, and whose writings
owed a tremendous authority to the name of their supposed
author, a direct disciple of St. Paul the Apostle.

The Platonic tradition during the Middle Ages, which
has been the subject of much recent study, followed again
three different lines of development.[7] In the Byzantine
East, the original works of Plato and of the Neoplatonists
were always available, and the study of Plato was surely
often combined with that of the ancient Greek poets and of
Aristotle.[8] The prevalence of Plato over Aristotle within
a synthesis of both was justified by Neoplatonic precedent,
and the tendency to harmonize Plato rather than Aristotle
with Christian theology was amply sanctioned by the Greek

patristic authors. In the eleventh century, Michael Psellus revived the interest in Platonic philosophy, and set an influential precedent by combining with it the *Chaldaic Oracles* attributed to Zoroaster, and the *Corpus Hermeticum*. In the fourteenth and fifteenth centuries, Gemistus Pletho attempted another revival of Plato's philosophy based on Proclus and Psellus. He even aimed at a philosophical reform of the falling Greek Empire, and gave, after the model of Proclus, an allegorical explanation of the Greek divinities, which exposed him to the charge that he wanted to restore ancient paganism.[9] Certainly he was convinced that Plato and his ancient followers were the representatives of a very old pagan theology which has for its witnesses the writings attributed to Hermes Trismegistus and Zoroaster, Orpheus and Pythagoras, and which parallels both in age and content the revelation of the Hebrew and Christian Scriptures. Through his teaching and writings, through his pupils, and through the violent reaction of his theological and Aristotelian opponents, Pletho did a good deal to awaken Platonic scholarship and philosophy in the Byzantine Empire during its last decades; and thanks to Pletho's stay in Italy and to the activities of his pupil, Cardinal Bessarion, and of other Greek scholars devoted or opposed to him, this development had important repercussions in the West until and beyond the end of the fifteenth century.[10]

Among the Arabs, Plato's position was inferior to that of Aristotle and consequently less important than in antiquity or in the Byzantine Middle Ages.[11] Whereas the corpus of Aristotle was almost completely translated into Arabic, only a few works of Plato, such as the *Republic*, the *Laws*, and the *Timaeus*, were made available, supplemented by a number of other Platonist writings. On the other hand, the Arabs derived many Platonist conceptions from the Aristotelian commentators, and they possessed at least two Aristotelian apocrypha, the *Liber de causis* and the *Theologia Aristotelis,* whose doctrinal content was based entirely on Proclus and Plotinus. Arabic philosophers such as Alfarabi wrote a paraphrase of Plato's *Laws,* and even the faithful Aristotelian commentator, Averroes, composed a paraphrase of Plato's *Republic.* Under the influence of the Arabic tradition, medieval Jewish thought included a strong neoplatonic current. Avicebron (ibn Gabirol), whose *Fountain of Life* exercised a strong influence in its Latin version also belongs to this tradition, and the peculiar form of medieval Jewish mysticism known as the Cabala contains several ideas derived from Neoplatonic and other late ancient philosophies.[12] Moreover, among both the Arabs and their Jewish disciples, the occult sciences of astrology, alchemy, and magic were cultivated in close connection with the genuine philosophical and scientific disciplines. These pseudo sciences also derived their traditions from the later phases of Greek antiquity, and they were or became associated with Platonist and Hermetic philosophy, with which they actually shared such notions as the world soul and the belief in the numerous hidden powers or specific affinities and antipathies of all things natural.

Roman antiquity, though poor in specific philosophical achievements, as we have seen, gave a larger share to the Platonic tradition than it did to Aristotle. Cicero, who had been a student at the Athenian Academy, reflected in his philosophical writings not only the Skepticism which had dominated that school for several centuries, but also the first phases of that eclectic or Middle Platonism which was just beginning to replace it. Further Middle Platonic ideas appear in Apuleius, occasionally in Seneca, and in Chalcidius' commentary on the *Timaeus;* whereas Neoplatonism was the basis for the writings of Macrobius, and for Boethius' influential *Consolation of Philosophy.* Of Plato's own works, the ancient Romans possessed only the partial versions of the *Timaeus* due to Cicero and Chalcidius; the version of Plotinus attributed to Victorinus was probably not extensive, and certainly did not survive very long. The most important representative of Platonism in ancient Latin literature was St. Augustine, who acknowledged his debt to Plato and Plotinus more frankly than most of his modern theological admirers.[13] Typical Platonist doctrines, such as the eternal presence of the universal forms in the mind of God, the immediate comprehension of these ideas by human reason, and the incorporeal nature and the immortality of the human soul, are persistently asserted in his earlier philosophical as well as in his later theological writings, and they do not become less Platonist because they are combined with different Biblical or specifically Augustinian conceptions or because Augustine rejected other Platonic or Neoplatonic doctrines that seemed incompatible with the Christian dogma. Augustine's repeated assertion that Platonism is closer to Christian doctrine than any other pagan philosophy went a long way to justify later attempts to combine or reconcile them with each other.

During the early Middle Ages, when philosophical studies were not much cultivated in Western Europe, the most important text translated from the Greek was the corpus of writings attributed to Dionysius the Areopagite, who was also identified with the patron saint of St. Denis near Paris.[14] And the only author who had philosophical significance, Johannes Scotus Eriugena, was strongly imbued with Neoplatonic conceptions which were accessible to him in their original Greek sources. When philosophical studies began to flourish with the rise of scholasticism after the middle of the eleventh century, Augustinianism, which comprised many Platonist elements, became the prevailing current. This was quite natural, since the writings of Augustine represented the most solid body of philosophical and theological ideas then available in Latin. It was supplemented by Boethius' *Consolation,* by his logical works and his translations from Aristotle and Porphyry, and by Chalcidius' partial translation and commentary of Plato's *Timaeus.* There was thus a body of source material available for philosophical study before the new translations from the Arabic and Greek were added, and this material was for the most part Platonist in character, and included at least one work of Plato, the *Timaeus.* Hence it is significant that in one of the most important centers of early scholasticism, at the cathedral school of Chartres, the *Timaeus* was apparently used as a textbook in natural philosophy, as a number of glosses and commentaries coming from that school would seem to indicate.[15] And a strange and long neglected Platonist work, the so-called *Altividius,* seems to have been composed during the same century.[16] When the new translations brought about a vast increase in philosophical and scientific literature, Aristotle and his commentators gradually gained the upper hand, as we have seen, and hence during the thirteenth century Aristotelianism became the prevailing current of Western thought. Yet at the same time, Platonism also profited from the new translating activity. The versions from the Greek included two dialogues of Plato, the *Phaedo* and the *Meno,* the work of Nemesius of Emesa, and a number of treatises by Proclus, such as the *Elements of Theology* and the commentary on the *Parmenides,* which contains part of Plato's own text.[17] On the other hand, we find among the versions from the Arabic not only the Aristotelian commentators who contained much Neoplatonic material, but also the *Liber de Causis,* Avicebron's *Fons vitae,* and a vast amount of astrological and alchemical literature that transmitted, or pretended to transmit, many notions of Platonist or Hermetic origin. Hence we are not surprised to find Augustinian or Neoplatonic notions even in the thought of many Aristotelian philosophers of the thirteenth and

early fourteenth centuries. On the other hand, the Augustinian tradition persisted as a secondary current during that
period, and the speculative mysticism of Master Eckhart
and his school drew much of its inspiration from the Areopagite, Proclus, and other Neoplatonic sources.

During the Renaissance, these medieval currents continued in many quarters. German speculative mysticism
was succeeded in the Low Countries by the more practical
Devotio Moderna which exercised a wide influence in
Northern Europe.[18] The Augustinian trend in theology and
metaphysics went on without interruption; the increasing
religious literature for laymen contained strong Augustinian elements, and even some of the Platonizing works written in Chartres during the twelfth century still found at-
tentive readers. Yet although several elements of medieval Platonism survived during the Renaissance, it would be
wrong to overlook the novel or different aspects of Renaissance Platonism. They were partly due to the impact of
Byzantine thought and learning, for the Eastern scholars
who came to Italy for a temporary or permanent residence
after the middle of the fourteenth century familiarized
their Western pupils with Plato's writings and teachings,
and with the controversy on the merits of Plato and Aristotle. While Chrysoloras was staying in Italy, he suggested
the first Latin translation of Plato's *Republic*. Pletho's
visit in Florence in 1438 left a deep impression, and the debate on Plato and Aristotle was continued in Italy by his
pupils and opponents and by their Western followers. The
most important document of the controversy is Bessarion's
defense of Plato which drew on Western sources and which
exercised some influence until the sixteenth century.[19] Other
documents related to this debate have but recently attracted
attention, or are still in need of further exploration.

Even more important was the impulse given by the
Italian humanists of the period. Petrarch was not well ac-

quainted with Plato's works or philosophy, but he was the first Western scholar who owned a Greek manuscript of Plato sent to him by a Byzantine colleague,[20] and in his attack on the authority of Aristotle among the philosophers of his time, he used at least Plato's name. This program was then carried out by his humanist successors. They studied Plato in the Greek original, and many of the dialogues were for the first time translated into Latin during the first half of the fifteenth century, including such works as the *Republic,* the *Laws,* the *Gorgias* and the *Phaedrus.* Some of these translations, like those of Leonardo Bruni, attained great popularity.[21] Other Platonist authors of antiquity were also made available in new Latin versions, and in the eclectic thought of the literary humanists Plato and his ancient followers occupied their appropriate place. Finally, at a time when a revival of everything ancient was the order of the day, and when restatements of many ancient philosophies were being attempted as a philosophical sequel to classical humanism, a revival of Platonism in one form or another was bound to occur.

However, Renaissance Platonism, in spite of its close links with classical humanism, cannot be understood as a mere part or offshoot of the humanistic movement. It possesses independent significance as a philosophical, not merely as a scholarly or literary, movement; it is connected both with the Augustinian and Aristotelian traditions of medieval philosophy; and thanks to the work of three major thinkers of the late fifteenth century, it became a major factor in the intellectual history of the sixteenth, and even afterwards. The earliest and greatest of the three, Nicolaus Cusanus, was indebted to German and Dutch mysticism as well as to Italian humanism.[22] In his philosophical thought, which has many original features, notions derived from Plato, Proclus, and the Areopagite play a major part. He interprets the ideas in the divine mind as a single archetype which expresses itself in each particular thing in a different way, and he stresses the certainty and exemplary status of pure mathematical knowledge, to mention only a few facets of his complex thought that show his link with the Platonic tradition. The most central and most influential representative of Renaissance Platonism is Marsilius Ficinus, in whom the medieval philosophical and religious heritage and the teachings of Greek Platonism are brought together in a novel synthesis.[28] As a translator, he gave to the West the first complete version of Plato and of Plotinus in Latin, adding several other Neoplatonic writings; and in adopting Pletho's conception of a pagan theological tradition before Plato, he translated also the works attributed to Pythagoras and Hermes Trismegistus that were bound to share the popularity and influence of Renaissance Platonism. In his *Platonic Theology* he gave to his contemporaries an authoritative summary of Platonist philosophy, in which the immortality of the soul is emphasized, reasserting to some extent the Thomist position against the Averroists. His Platonic Academy with its courses and discussions provided for some decades an institutional center whose influence was spread all over Europe through his letters and other writings. Assigning to the human soul the central place in the hierarchy of the universe, he gave a metaphysical expression to a notion dear to his humanist predecessors; whereas his doctrine of spiritual love in Plato's sense, for which he coined the term Platonic love, became one of the most popular concepts of later Renaissance literature. His emphasis on the inner ascent of the soul towards God through contemplation links him with the mystics, whereas his doctrine of the unity of the world brought about by the soul influenced the natural philosophers of the sixteenth century.

Closely associated with the Florentine Academy, but in many ways different from Ficino, was his younger contemporary, Giovanni Pico della Mirandola.[24] In his thought, which did not reach full maturity, the attempt was made to achieve a synthesis between Platonism and Aristotelianism. His curiosity encompassed also Arabic and Hebrew language and thought, and as the first Western scholar who became acquainted with the Jewish Cabala, he made the influential attempt to reconcile the Cabala with Christian theology and to associate it with the Platonist tradition. His *Oration* on the dignity of man became the most famous expression of that humanist credo to which he gave a novel philosophical interpretation in terms of man's freedom to choose his own destiny.[25]

The place of Platonism in sixteenth-century thought is rather complex and difficult to describe.[26] Unlike humanism or Aristotelianism, it was not identified with the teaching traditions in the literary or philosophical disciplines, and its institutional connections were slender and somewhat uncertain. Some of Plato's dialogues were among the standard prose texts that were read in all courses in Greek at the universities and secondary schools of the period, and this accounted for a wide diffusion of his philosophical ideas. In the academies — a new type of institution, half learned society and half literary club, which flourished especially in Italy throughout the century and afterwards — lectures and courses on the so-called philosophy of love, often based on Platonizing poems and always influenced by Plato's *Symposium* and its commentators, were a common feature, especially in Florence, where the memory of Ficino's Academy was never forgotten. Yet Francesco Patrizi's attempts to introduce courses on Platonic philosophy at the universities of Ferrara and Rome were of short duration, and a similar course given for several decades at Pisa was entrusted to scholars who taught Aristotle at the same time and thus were led to compare and to combine Plato with Aristotle, rather than to give him an undivided allegiance.

Nevertheless it would be a mistake to underestimate the importance of sixteenth-century Platonism, or to overlook its almost ubiquitous presence, often combined with humanism or Aristotelianism or other trends or ideas, but always recognizable in its own distinctive physiognomy. In the course of the century, the works of Plato and of the ancient Platonists, and the connected writings attributed to Orpheus and Zoroaster, to Hermes and the Pythagoreans, were all printed and reprinted in the Greek original and in Latin translations, and likewise the writings of the Renaissance Platonists such as Cusanus, Ficino, and Pico were widely read and diffused, and some of this material even found its way into the vernacular languages, especially French and Italian. By that time, this body of literature supplied scholars and readers with the largest and most substantial alternative for, or supplement to, the works of Aristotle and his commentators. No wonder that its impact was felt in many fields and areas of thought and of learning, although it would be difficult, if not impossible, to bring these various facets of Platonism under one common denominator, or to establish very precise relationships among them.

Among the philosophers we find some who would try to combine Plato and Aristotle, like Francesco Verino, Jacopo Mazzoni, and the Frenchman Jacobus Carpentarius, best known for his sinister role during the Massacre of St. Bartholomew. Others professed their undivided allegiance to Plato, like Francesco da Diacceto, Ficino's successor in Florence, and the Spaniard Sebastian Fox Morcillo, and the greatest of all, Francesco Patrizi. Yet the influence of Plato and Platonism extended far beyond the circle of those who wanted to be known as followers of that tradition. The natural philosophers of the time who are best known for their original speculations, like Paracelsus, Telesio, or Bruno, were strongly indebted to the Platonic tradition. Telesio, who distinguishes between two souls, is a thorough empiricist when dealing with the lower soul, to which he assigns our ordinary functions and activities, but follows the Platonists in his treatment of the higher, immortal soul. And Bruno is a Platonist not only in his *Heroic Enthusiasts,* where he develops a theory of love derived from the *Symposium* and its interpreters, but also in his metaphysics, where he borrows his concept of the world soul from Plotinus and follows Cusanus on other important points.[27] The broad stream of astrological and alchemical literature, which continued and even increased during the sixteenth century, also presupposes such notions as a world soul or the inner powers and affinities of things celestial, elementary, and composite, notions that go back to Arabic sources that were still widely used in these circles, but which derived new impetus and dignity from the Greek and modern Platonist writers and from the Hermetic works associated with them. On the other hand, we note that certain Aristotelian philosophers like Nifo, who wanted to defend the immortality of the soul, made use of the arguments given in Plato's *Phaedo* or in Ficino's *Platonic Theology,* and that even the more "naturalistic" among the Renaissance Aristotelians, like Pomponazzi or Cremonini, were willing to accept certain specific Platonist doctrines. For the humanists unfriendly to the Aristotelian tradition, Plato and his school always held much attraction. John Colet was much impressed by the Areopagite, and we have just received direct evidence that he was in touch with Marsilio Ficino.[28] Sir Thomas More translated the life and a few letters of Pico into English, and his noted *Utopia,* however original in its content, could hardly have been conceived without the reading of Plato's *Republic.*[29] Erasmus, in the *Enchiridion* and the later part of the *Praise of Folly,* endorsed a somewhat diluted form of Platonism when he opposed the higher folly of the inner spiritual life to the lower folly of ordinary existence, and Peter Ramus used at least the name of Plato in his bold attempt to replace the traditional Aristotelian logic of the schools. In France, scholars like Lefèvre d'Etaples, Charles de Bouelles, Symphorien Champier, and others received many of their ideas from Cusanus and Ficinus,[30] Pico apparently affected Zwingli,[31] and his Christian cabalism was adopted by Reuchlin and by many other Platonizing theologians.[32] A few scholars have even discovered Platonist elements in the theology of Calvin.[33] Theologians like Ambrosius Flandinus, who opposed both Pomponazzi and Luther, composed commentaries on Plato, or like Aegidius of Viterbo, general of the Augustinian Hermits, wrote a commentary on the Sentences "ad mentem Platonis."[34] When the Lateran Council of 1513 condemned Averroes' unity of the intellect and promulgated the immortality of the soul as an official dogma of the Church, we are inclined to see in this event an effect of Renaissance Platonism upon Catholic theology, especially since the Platonist Aegidius of Viterbo endorsed and perhaps inspired the decision, whereas the leading Thomist, Caietanus, opposed it,[35] since he departed on this issue, as on some others, from the position of Aquinas, and held with Pomponazzi that the immortality of the soul could not be demonstrated. Aside from the professional theologians, religious writers and poets like Marguerite of Navarre, the poets of the Lyon circle or Joachim Du Bellay were impressed by the Platonist appeal to contemplation and inner experience.[36] Ficino's notion of Platonic love, that is, of the spiritual love for another human being that is but a disguised love of the soul for God, and some of his other concepts, found favor with such contemporary poets as Lorenzo de' Medici and Girolamo Benivieni, and this Platonizing poetry had among its successors in the sixteenth century Michelangelo and Spenser, besides many minor Italian, French, and English authors in whom the Platonist element is not always easy to distinguish from the common pattern of "Petrarchism."[37] It is not correct to say, as do some scholars, that Dante, Guido Cavalcanti, or Petrarch were poets of Platonic love, but they were thus interpreted by Ficino, Landino, and others, and thus it was possible for their imitators in the sixteenth century to merge their style and imagery with those of the genuine Platonist tradition. Ficino's doctrine of Platonic love was repeated and developed not only in many sonnets and other poems of the sixteenth century, but also in a large body of prose literature which grew up around the literary academies and became fashionable with the reading public: the *trattati d'amore*.[38] These dialogues or treatises discuss in different forms the nature and beneficial effects of spiritual love in the Platonist manner, and also a variety of related Platonist doctrines like the immortality of the soul or the existence and knowledge of the pure Ideas. Among the numerous authors who contributed to this literature and who tended to popularize but also to dilute the teachings of Platonism, we find, besides many now forgotten, such influential writers as Bembo and Castiglione, for whom Platonist philosophy was but a passing fancy, and also a poet like Tasso, whose philosophical prose writings have not yet been sufficiently studied, and such serious philosophers as Francesco da Diacceto, Leone Ebreo, and Francesco Patrizi. Giordano Bruno's *Eroici Furori* also belongs in this tradition, and may be better understood against this background. Finally Plato's doctrine of divine madness as expressed in the *Ion* and *Phaedrus* appealed to many poets and literary critics who would either add this Platonic doctrine to an otherwise Aristotelian system of poetics, or use it as the cornerstone of an anti-Aristotelian theory, as was done by Patrizi.[39]

In the theory of painting and of the other visual arts, which was not yet combined with poetics in a single system of aesthetics, as happened in the eighteenth century,[40] the analogy between the conceptions of the artist and the ideas of the divine creator which appears in Cicero, Seneca, Plotinus, and other Middle and Neoplatonic authors was adopted by Duerer and by many later critics.[41] Moreover, the expression of philosophical ideas of Platonist origin has been discussed and partly established in the iconography of the works of such masters as Botticelli, Raphael, and Michelangelo.[42] If we pass from the visual arts to the theory of music, which in the sixteenth century constituted a separate branch of literature unrelated to poetics or the theory of painting, we notice again that Plato is praised and cited by Francesco Gafurio, by Vincenzo Galileo, the father of the great scientist, and by other musical theorists of the time.[43] The extent of this "musical Platonism" has not been investigated, and its precise links with the philosophical tradition remain to be defined. Yet it is worth noting that Ficino was an enthusiastic amateur in music, and wrote several shorter treatises on musical theory. It is conceivable and even probable that the passages on musical proportions in Plato's *Timaeus,* together with Ficino's extensive commentary on them, made a strong impression on those professional musicians who had a literary education and were familiar with the fame and authority of Plato and his school.

Of even greater interest is the impact of Renaissance Platonism upon the sciences, a subject that has been much debated by recent historians. Again, a distinction must be made between the different sciences, which then as now differed so much in method, subject matter, sources, and traditions. Obviously, the history of technology and engineering would show no traces of Platonist, or for that matter of Aristotelian, influence.[44] In natural history also, where the Aristotelian tradition prevailed, Platonism hardly made itself felt. Yet in medicine, astrological and alchemical theories exercised a good deal of influence during that time,

and the medical writings of Ficino, which embodied some
of his philosophical and astrological views, were widely
read, especially in Germany. Yet the main impact of
Platonism, as might be expected, was felt in the mathematical sciences, which had been most cultivated and respected
by Plato and his followers.[45] Mathematicians who were
concerned with the theoretical and philosophical status of
their science, and philosophers who wanted to emphasize
the certainty and importance of mathematical knowledge,
would be inclined to recur either to the number symbolism
of the Pythagoreans that had been associated with Platonism since late antiquity, or to the belief in the nonempirical
a priori validity and certainty of mathematical concepts and
propositions that goes back to Plato himself and that had
been reëmphasized by some, though not by all, representatives of the Platonic tradition.   This belief was shared but
not emphasized by Plotinus or Ficino, who were more concerned with other features of the Platonic tradition, but it
was strongly expressed and applied by Cusanus.   In the sixteenth century when the doctrines of Plato and Aristotle
were compared with each other, the superiority of quantitative over qualitative knowledge was considered one of the
characteristic points of the Platonic position, and against
this background it is quite significant that the Platonist
Patrizi emphasized the theoretical priority and superiority
of mathematics over physics.[46] This position had great po-
tentialities at a time when mathematics was rapidly prog-
ressing, and when the question arose whether the qualitative
physics of the Aristotelian tradition should be replaced by
a quantitative physics based on mathematics and in a way
reducible to it.   Hence there is no wonder that some of the
founders of modern physical science should have been attracted by at least this feature of Platonism.   In the case of
Kepler, no doubt seems possible that his cosmology is
rooted in Renaissance Platonism, from which he borrowed

not only his mathematical conception of the universe but also his notion of cosmic harmony, and at least in his earlier period, his belief in number symbolism and astrology. To understand the validity of Kepler's laws of planetary motion, the modern student of astronomy does not need to be concerned with his Platonist cosmology. Yet the historian of science will do well to recognize that the positive scientific discoveries of the past were never unrelated to the theoretical and philosophical assumptions of the investigating scientist, whether they were true or false from our point of view, whether consciously expressed or tacitly accepted by him. Even if we want to say that Kepler discovered his laws in spite of, and not on account of, his Platonist cosmology, as historians we cannot be concerned only with those parts of his work and thought that have been accepted as true by later scientists, but we must also understand his errors as well, as an integral part of his scientific and philosophical thought. Otherwise, the history of science becomes nothing but a catalogue of disconnected facts, and a modern version of hagiography.

Whereas Kepler's link with the Platonic tradition has been generally admitted, though frequently regretted, the question of Galileo's Platonism has been a more controversial matter.[47] It has been pointed out that, on account of his known dislike for the Aristotelian tradition, he tended to attribute to Aristotle views which he opposed and which are not always consistent with each other or with the text of Aristotle. It also must be admitted that he borrowed much more from that tradition than one might expect, including such important notions as the distinction between analysis and synthesis in the method of scientific knowledge. His atomism and his distinction between primary and secondary qualities is ultimately derived from Democritus, and his conviction that mathematical relations can be exactly reproduced by material conditions is radically opposed to

Plato. On the other hand, his claims for the absolute certainty of mathematical knowledge are truly Platonic, and his demand that nature should be understood in quantitative, mathematical terms is no less in line with the Platonist position of his time because he rejects the Pythagorean number symbolism often associated with it. Finally, in the famous passage where he also refers to Plato's theory of reminiscence, he states not merely that first principles are evident without demonstration, as any Aristotelian would have granted, but that they are spontaneously known and produced by the human mind, which is specifically Platonic.[48] The fact that there are Aristotelian, Democritean, and novel elements in Galileo's thought does not disprove that Platonic notions are also present in it, and as long as we are inclined to attribute any significance to these latter notions, we are entitled to assign to Galileo a place in the history of Platonism.

With the beginning of a new period of philosophical and scientific thought in the seventeenth century, the Platonic tradition ceases to dominate the development as a separate movement, but continues to influence a number of secondary currents and the thought of many leading thinkers. In the case of Descartes, his indebtedness to scholastic terminology and arguments is now generally admitted, but it has also been shown, though this is less widely known, that he borrowed important elements in ethics from the Stoics, and in epistemology and metaphysics from Platonism.[49] Spinoza's thought contains many Platonist elements, and his notion of the intellectual love of God has been connected with the love speculation of the Renaissance, and especially with Leone Ebreo. It is even easier to point out the Platonizing elements in Malebranche, Leibniz, Kant, and Goethe. Even England, where the prevailing philosophical and scientific tradition seems to be represented by Bacon, Locke, and Hume, by Boyle and Newton, produced in the seventeenth century a group of interesting thinkers, the so-called Cambridge Platonists, who professed their allegiance to Platonism and actually constitute the most important phase of professed Platonism after the Florentine Academy.[50] Thus it is not surprising to find strong Platonizing tendencies in the late Berkeley, in Shaftesbury, and in Coleridge, authors who in turn exercised a rather wide influence.

Thus I hope that it has become apparent that Renaissance Platonism, in spite of its complex and somewhat elusive nature, was an important phenomenon both for its own period and for the subsequent centuries down to 1800. We must resign ourselves to the fact that in most cases the Platonist elements of thought are combined with doctrines of a different origin and character, and that even the professed Platonists did not express the thought of Plato in its purity, as modern scholars understand it, but combined it with more or less similar notions that had accrued to it in late antiquity, the Middle Ages, or more recent times. Yet if we understand Platonism with these qualifications and in a broad and flexible sense, it was a powerful intellectual force throughout the centuries, and we shall understand its nature best if we realize that until the rise of modern Plato scholarship, Plato appealed to his readers not only through the content of his inimitable dialogues, but also through the diverse and often complicated ideas which his commentators and followers down to the sixteenth and seventeenth centuries had associated with him.

4. PAGANISM AND CHRISTIANITY

YOU MIGHT easily raise the question whether the problem which I propose to discuss in this lecture is relevant to the general topic of this series, and there is no doubt that I feel quite unequipped to deal with it appropriately. Yet although philosophical thought has its own distinctive core which ought to be always considered in its own terms, its history in a broader sense can rarely be understood without taking into account the religious as well as the scientific and literary currents of a particular age. In the period which we have been discussing in these lectures, religious events such as the Protestant and Catholic Reformations were of such momentous importance, and their significance in relation to the Renaissance has been the subject of so much debate, that even a short and superficial account of Renaissance thought would be incomplete without some consideration of the Reformation. Some scholars have seemingly avoided this problem by treating the Reformation as a new epoch, different from, and in a sense opposed to, the Renaissance. We prefer to consider the Reformation as an important development within the broader historical period which extended at least to the end of the sixteenth century, and which we continue to call, with certain qualifications, the Renaissance. Obviously, it cannot be our task to describe the original contributions made by the reformers to religious thought, let alone the changes in ecclesiastic institutions brought about by their initiative, or the political and social factors which accounted for their popularity and success. In accordance with our general topic, we shall merely try to understand in which ways, positive or negative, the classicism of the Renaissance exercised an influence upon the religious thought of the period, and especially upon the Reformation.

Many historians of the last century tended to associate the Italian Renaissance and Italian humanism with some kind of irreligion, and to interpret the Protestant and Catholic Reformations as expressions of a religious revival which challenged and finally defeated the un-Christian culture of the preceding period.[1] The moral ideas and literary allegories in the writings of the humanists were taken to be expressions, real or potential, overt or concealed, of a new paganism incompatible with Christianity. The neat separation between reason and faith advocated by the Aristotelian philosophers was considered as a hypocritical device to cover up a secret atheism, whereas the emphasis on a natural religion common to all men, found in the work of the Platonists and Stoics, was characterized as pantheism.[2] This picture of the supposed paganism of the Renaissance which was drawn by historians with much horror or enthusiasm, depending on the strength of their religious or irreligious convictions, can partly be dismissed as the result of later legends and preconceptions. In part, it may be traced to charges made against the humanists and philosophers by hostile or narrow-minded contemporaries, which should not be accepted at their face value.[3] Most recent historians have taken quite a different view of the matter.[4] There was, to be sure, a good deal of talk about the pagan gods and heroes in the literature of the Renaissance, and it was justified by the familiar device of allegory, and strengthened by the belief in astrology, but there were few, if any, thinkers who seriously thought of reviving ancient pagan cults. The word pantheism had not yet been invented,[5] and although the word atheism was generously used in polemics during the later sixteenth century,[6] there were probably no real atheists and barely a few pantheists during the Renaissance. The best or worst we may say is that there were some thinkers who might be considered, or actually were considered, as forerunners of eighteenth-century free thought.   There was then, of course, as there was before and afterwards, a certain amount of religious indifference and of merely nominal adherence to the doctrines of the Church.   There were many cases of conduct in private and public life that were not in accordance with the moral commands of Christianity, and there were plenty of abuses in ecclesiastic practice itself, but I am not inclined to consider this as distinctive of the Renaissance period.

The real core of the tradition concerning Renaissance paganism is something quite different: it is the steady and irresistible growth of nonreligious intellectual interests which were not so much opposed to the content of religious doctrine, as rather competing with it for individual and public attention.   This was nothing fundamentally new, but rather a matter of degree and of emphasis.   The Middle Ages was certainly a religious epoch, but it would be wrong to assume that men's entire attention was occupied by religious, let alone by theological, preoccupations.   Medieval architects built castles and palaces, not only cathedrals and monasteries.   Even when the clerics held the monopoly of learning, they cultivated grammar and the other liberal arts besides theology, and during the High Middle Ages, when specialization began to arise, nonreligious literature also expanded.   The thirteenth century produced not Thomas Aquinas alone, as some people seem to believe, or other scholastic theologians, but also a vast literature on Roman law, medicine, Aristotelian logic and physics, mathematics and astronomy, letter-writing and rhetoric, and even on classical Latin poetry, not to mention the chronicles and histories, the lyric and epic poetry in Latin and in the vernacular languages.   This development made further progress during the Renaissance period, as a glance at the inventory of a manuscript collection or at a bibliography of printed books will easily reveal, and it continued unchecked during and after the Reformation, whatever the theologians of that time or later times may have felt about it. If an age where the nonreligious concerns that had been growing for centuries attained a kind of equilibrium with religious and theological thought, or even began to surpass it in vitality and appeal, must be called pagan, the Renaissance was pagan, at least in certain places and phases. Yet since the religious convictions of Christianity were either retained or transformed, but never really challenged, it seems more appropriate to call the Renaissance a fundamentally Christian age.

To prove this point, it would be pertinent in the first place to state that the medieval traditions of religious thought and literature continued without interruption until and after the Reformation, and that Italy was no exception to this rule. The study of theology and canon law, and the literary production resulting from it, tended to increase rather than to decline, a fact that is often overlooked because historians of these subjects have paid less attention to that period than to the earlier ones, except for the material directly connected with the Reformation controversies. German mysticism was succeeded during the very period with which we are concerned by the more practical and less speculative *Devotio Moderna* in the Low Countries, a movement that produced such an important document as the *Imitation of Christ,* contributed to a reform of secondary education all over Northern Europe, and had a formative influence on such thinkers as Cusanus and Erasmus.[7] Effective preachers made a deep impression on the learned and unlearned alike all over fifteenth-century Italy, and sometimes led to revivalist movements and political repercussions, of which Savonarola is the most famous but by no means an isolated instance.[8] In Italy no less than in the rest of Europe, the religious guilds directed the activities of the laity and exercised a tremendous influence upon the visual arts, music, and literature.[9] Partly in connection with these guilds, an extensive religious literature of a popular character was circulated, which was composed either by clerics or by laymen, but always addressed to the latter and usually in the vernacular languages. These facts, along with the persistence of church doctrine, institutions, and worship, would go a long way to prove the religious preoccupations of the Renaissance period.

Yet we are not so much concerned with the undoubted survival of medieval Christianity in the Renaissance as with the changes and transformations which affected religious thought during that period. As a distinguished historian has put it,[10] Christianity is not only medieval, but also ancient and modern, and thus it was possible for Christian thought during the Renaissance to cease being medieval in many respects, and yet to remain Christian. This novelty is apparent in the new doctrines and institutions created by the Protestant and Catholic Reformations, a topic on which I shall not attempt to elaborate. I shall merely show that the humanist movement, as we have tried to describe it in our first lecture, had its share in bringing about those changes in religious thought.

The view that the humanist movement was essentially pagan or anti-Christian cannot be sustained. It was successfully refuted by the humanists themselves when they defended their work and program against the charges of unfriendly theologians of their own time. The opposite view, which has had influential defenders in recent years, namely that Renaissance humanism was in its origin a religious movement,[11] or even a religious reaction against certain antireligious tendencies in the Middle Ages,[12] seems to me equally wrong or exaggerated. I am convinced that humanism was in its core neither religious nor antireligious, but a literary and scholarly orientation that could be and, in many cases, was pursued without any explicit discourse on religious topics by individuals who otherwise might be fervent or nominal members of one of the Christian churches. On the other hand, there were many scholars and thinkers with a humanist training who had a genuine concern for religious and theological problems, and it is my contention that the way they brought their humanist training to bear upon the source material and subject matter of Christian theology was one of the factors responsible for the changes which Christianity underwent during that period. The most important elements in the humanist approach to religion and theology were the attack upon the scholastic method and the emphasis upon the return to the classics, which in this case meant the Christian classics, that is, the Bible and the Church Fathers.

In order to understand the significance of these attitudes, we must once more go back to antiquity and the Middle Ages. Christianity originated in a Jewish Palestine which had become politically a part of the Roman Empire, and culturally a part of the Hellenistic world. At the time when the new religion began to spread through the Mediterranean area, its sacred writings which were to form the canon of the New Testament were composed in Greek, that is, in a language which showed the marks of a long literary and philosophical tradition, and in part by authors such as Paul, Luke, and John, who had enjoyed a literary and perhaps a philosophical education. In the following centuries, the early Apologists, the Greek Fathers, and the great Councils were engaged in the task of defining and developing Christian doctrine, and of making it acceptable to the entire Greek-speaking world. Thus the reading and study of the Greek poets and prose writers was finally approved, with some reservations, whereas the teachings of the Greek philosophical schools were subjected to careful examination, rejecting everything that seemed incompatible with Christian doctrine, but using whatever appeared compatible to bolster and to supplement Christian theology. After the precedent of Philo the Jew, Clement of Alexandria and the other Greek Fathers went a long way in adding Greek philosophical methods and notions, especially Stoic and Platonist, to the doctrinal, historical and institutional teachings contained in the Bible, and in creating out of these diverse elements a novel and coherent Christian view of God, the universe, and man. At the same time, a similar synthesis of ancient and Christian elements was achieved by the Latin Fathers of the Western Church. Writers like Arnobius, Cyprian, Lactantius, and Ambrose embody in their writings the best grammatical and rhetorical training, based on the Roman poets and orators, that was available in their time. Jerome added to his consummate Latin literary education that Greek and Hebrew scholarship which enabled him to translate the entire Bible from the original languages into Latin. Augustine, the most important and complex of them all, was not only an excellent and cultured rhetorician according to the standards of his time, but also made use of the allegorical method to justify the study of the ancient Roman poets and prose writers.[13] Furthermore, Augustine was a learned and productive philosophical and theological thinker, who left to posterity a substantial body of writings in which traditional religious doctrine was enriched with novel theological ideas like the City of God, original sin, and predestination, and also with philosophical conceptions of Greek and especially Neoplatonic origin, like the eternal forms in the divine mind, the incorporeality and immortality of the soul, conceptions which appear more prominently in his earlier, philosophical writings, but which he did not completely abandon even in his later years when he was engaged in Church administration and in theological controversies with the heretics of his time. Thus Christianity, during the first six centuries of its existence, which still belong to the period of classical antiquity, absorbed a large amount of Greek philosophical ideas and of Greek and Latin literary traditions, so that some historians have been able to speak, with a certain amount of justification, of the humanism of the Church Fathers. In recent years, it has become customary among theologians and historians to ignore or to minimize the indebtedness of Philo, Augustine, and the other early Christian writers to Greek philosophy.[14] I must leave it to the judgment of present-day theologians and their followers whether they are really serving their cause by trying to eliminate from Christian theology all notions originally derived from Greek philosophy. Certainly those historians who follow a similar tendency and deny the significance of Greek philosophy for early Christian thought can be corrected through an objective study of the sources.

During the early Middle Ages, the Latin West had very limited philosophical and scientific interests, as we have seen, but it continued as best it could the grammatical and theological studies sanctioned by Augustine and the other Latin Fathers; and a number of Spanish, Irish, Anglo-Saxon and Carolingian scholars achieved distinction in this way. In the history of theology, a marked change from the pattern of the patristic period occurred with the rise of scholasticism after the eleventh century.[15] What was involved was not merely the influx of additional philosophical sources and ideas, both Platonist and Aristotelian, of which we have spoken in the preceding lectures. Much more important was the novel tendency to transform the subject matter of Christian theology into a topically arranged and logically coherent system. There was no precedent for this either in the Bible or in Latin patristic literature, although certain Greek writers like Origen and John of Damascus had paved the way. The desire for a topical arrangement found its expression in the collections of sen-

tences and church canons which culminated in the twelfth
century in the *Libri Sententiarum* of Peter Lombard and
the *Decretum* of Gratian which for many centuries were to
serve as the standard textbooks of theology and of canon
law. At the same time, the rising interest in Aristotelian
logic led to the endeavor, first cultivated in the schools of
Bec, Laon, and Paris, to apply the newly refined methods
of dialectical argument to the subject matter of theology,
which thus became by the standards of the time a real science. It is this method of Anselm, Abelard, and Peter
Lombard which dominates the theological tradition of the
high and later Middle Ages, including Bonaventura, Aquinas, Duns Scotus, and Ockham, not the older method of
Peter Damiani or St. Bernard, who tried in vain to stem the
rising tide of scholasticism and whose influence was hence
confined to the more popular and practical, less scientific
areas of later religious literature.

If we remember these facts concerning the history of
theology in the West, we can understand what it meant for
a Renaissance humanist with religious convictions to attack
scholastic theology and to advocate a return to the Biblical
and patristic sources of Christianity. It meant that these
sources, which after all were themselves the product of
antiquity, were considered as the Christian classics which
shared the prestige and authority of classical antiquity and
to which the same methods of historical and philological
scholarship could be applied.[16] Thus Petrarch shuns the
medieval theologians except St. Bernard and quotes only
early Christian writers in his religious and theological re-
marks.[17] Valla laments the harmful influence of logic and
philosophy upon theology and advocates an alliance between faith and eloquence. And Erasmus repeatedly attacks the scholastic theologians and emphasizes that the
early Christian writers were grammarians, but no dialecti-
cians. In his rejection of scholastic theology and his em-

phasis on the authority of Scripture and the Fathers, even
Luther no less than John Colet is in agreement with the
humanists, whereas the attempt to combine the study of
theology with an elegant Latin style and a thorough knowledge of the Greek and Latin classics characterizes not only
many Italian humanists and Erasmus, but also Melanchthon, Calvin,[18] and the early Jesuits.

If we try to assess the positive contributions of humanist scholarship to Renaissance theology, we must emphasize
above all their achievements in what we might call sacred
philology.[19] Valla led the way with his notes on the New
Testament, in which he criticized several passages of Jerome's Vulgate on the basis of the Greek text. He was followed by Manetti, who made a new translation of the New
Testament from Greek into Latin and of the Psalms from
Hebrew into Latin, a work which has not yet been sufficiently studied.[20] Erasmus' edition of the Greek New Testament is well known. It is this humanist tradition of biblical
philology which provides the background and method for
Luther's German version of the entire Bible from the
Hebrew and Greek, as well as for the official revision of
the Vulgate accomplished by Catholic scholars during the
second half of the sixteenth century,[21] and for the official
English version completed under King James I. The theological exegesis of the Bible and of its various parts had
always been an important branch of Christian literature
ever since patristic times. It was temporarily overshad-
owed, though by no means eliminated, by the predomi-
nance of Peter Lombard's *Sentences* in the theological
curriculum of the later Middle Ages, but it derived new
force in the sixteenth century from the emphasis of Protestant theology upon the original source of Christian doctrine. To what extent the exegesis of that period was affected by the new methods and standards of humanist

philology, seems to be a question which has not yet been sufficiently investigated.[22]

An even wider field was offered to humanist scholarship by the large body of Greek Christian literature of the patristic and Byzantine period. Some of this material had been translated into Latin towards the end of antiquity and again during the twelfth century. Yet it is an established fact not sufficiently known or appreciated that a large proportion of Greek patristic literature was for the first time translated into Latin by the humanists and humanistically trained theologians of the fifteenth and sixteenth centuries.[23] This applies to many important writings of Eusebius, Basil, and John Chrysostom, of Gregory of Nazianzus and of Nyssa, not to mention many later or lesser authors, or the writings which had been known before and were now reissued in presumably better Latin versions. Early in the fifteenth century, Leonardo Bruni translated Basil's letter which defended the reading of the pagan poets on the part of Christian students, and this welcome support of the humanist program by a distinguished Church author attained such a wide circulation that we may assume that it was used in the classroom.[24] About the same time, Ambrogio Traversari, a monk with a classical training, dedicated a considerable amount of his energy to the translating of Greek Christian writers, thus setting an example to many later scholars, clerics, and laymen alike. These Latin versions attained great popularity as the numerous manuscript copies and printed editions may prove. They were often followed by vernacular translations, and in the sixteenth century, by editions of the original Greek texts. Thus we must conclude that the Renaissance possessed a much better and more complete knowledge of Greek Christian literature and theology than the preceding age, and it would be an interesting question, which to my knowledge has not yet been explored, whether or to what extent the newly diffused ideas of these Greek authors exercised an influence on the theological discussions and controversies of the Reformation period.

Whereas a considerable proportion of Greek Christian literature was thus made available to the West through the labors of the humanists, the writings of the Latin Church Fathers had been continuously known through the Middle Ages, and never ceased to exercise a strong influence on all theologians and other writers. Yet in this area also humanist scholarship brought about significant changes. The humanists were fully aware of the fact that authors like Ambrose and Lactantius, and especially Jerome and Augustine, belong to the good period of ancient Latin literature, and hence must be considered as "Christian classics." Consequently, some of their works were included in the curriculum of the humanistic school, as in that of Guarino,[25] and regularly listed as recommended readings by humanist educators like Bruni, Valla, Erasmus, and Vives. Thus the Latin Fathers were read in the humanistic period no less than before, but they were grouped with the classical Latin writers rather than with the medieval theologians, and this fact could not fail to bring about a change in the way in which they were read and understood.

Moreover, the new philological methods of editing and commenting which the humanists had developed in their studies of the ancient authors were also applied to the Latin Church Fathers. We know in the case of Augustine that many manuscript copies and printed editions of the fifteenth century were due to the efforts of humanist scholars, and that Vives composed a philological commentary on the City of God, with which he was said in true humanist fashion to have restored St. Augustine to his ancient integrity. The application of humanist scholarship to Latin patristic literature culminated in the work of Erasmus, who prepared for a number of the most important writers criti-

cal editions of their collected works. His example was followed by Protestant and Catholic scholars alike, and later
in the sixteenth century, the pope appointed a special com-
mittee of scholars for the purpose of publishing the writings of the Fathers in new critical editions.[26]

Another field in which humanist scholarship was applied
to the problems which concerned the churches and theologians was the study of ecclesiastic history. The critical
methods developed by the humanists for the writing of ancient and medieval history on the basis of authentic contemporary documents and evidence were first applied to church
history by Valla in his famous attack on the Donation of
Constantine. In the sixteenth century, the Magdeburg
Centuriatores used this method to rewrite the whole history
of the church from the Protestant point of view, and later
in the century, Cardinal Baronius and his assistants under-
took the same task for the Catholic side.[27]

The humanist interest in early Christian literature was
not limited to philological and historical preoccupations,
but also had its doctrinal consequences in philosophy and
theology. Just as the philological study of the pagan
philosophers led the way towards a revival of Platonism
and of other ancient philosophies, and more specifically to
a new kind of Aristotelianism, so the humanistic study of
the Bible and of the Church Fathers led to new interpretations of early Christian thought, that are characteristic
of the Renaissance and Reformation period. Thus the attempt to interpret the Epistles of Paul without the context
and superstructure of scholastic theology was made by
scholars like Ficino, Colet, and Erasmus before it had such
powerful and decisive results in the work of Luther.[28] Even
more significant and more widespread was the influence exercised during the Renaissance by St. Augustine, and hence
I should like to discuss, as briefly as possible, some aspects
of Renaissance Augustinianism.[29]

The terms "Augustinianism" or "the Augustinian tradition" cover almost as many different meanings as the term "Platonism," since a thinker may be called an Augustinian for many different reasons. The cause of this ambiguity is the same as in the case of Plato: the great variety and complexity of Augustine's work. Before he had become a bishop and a dogmatic theologian, Augustine had been a rhetorician, a philosopher, and a heretic who underwent a conversion, and all these elements and experiences left their traces in his writings. Augustine is a preacher, a moral teacher, and a political thinker, an expositor of the Bible, an autobiographer, a skeptic and neoplatonic philosopher, a rhetorically trained writer who finds a justification for the study of the pagan poets, a systematic theologian who continues the work of the Greek Fathers, a vigorous opponent of heresies who formulated or sharpened the doctrines of original sin, grace, and predestination. All these elements were potential sources of inspiration for later readers of Augustine's works.

During the early Middle Ages, Augustine's influence was chiefly felt in the fields of theology proper, education, and political thought. During the rise of scholasticism in the eleventh and twelfth centuries, Augustine's works supplied the chief philosophical and theological inspiration, and most of the early scholastics have been rightly called Augustinians. During the thirteenth and fourteenth centuries when Aristotle became predominant among the philosophers and theologians, Augustinianism survived as an important secondary current, and even the Aristotelians preserved many traces of Augustinian influence. At the same time, the theology of the mystics, and the broad stream of popular religious literature remained unaffected by Aristotle and faithful to the spirit of Augustine.

The influence of Augustine during the Renaissance period followed in part the same lines taken during the preceding centuries. The Augustinian current in scholastic _nilosophy and theology can be traced through the fifteenth century and afterwards, and the popular religious literature affected by his ideas increased in volume during the same period. Among the leaders of the _Devotio Moderna_ in the Low Countries, after the Bible Augustine was the leading authority, as he had been with St. Bernard and the German mystics.

Yet besides these traditional lines of Augustinian influence whose importance should not be underestimated, we also note certain attitudes towards Augustine that seem to be of a different type. For Petrarch, who ignores and dislikes scholastic theology but always emphasizes his religious convictions, Augustine was one of the favorite authors who even exercised a decisive influence upon his spiritual development. Aside from numerous citations, two instances deserve special mention. When Petrarch composed his most personal work, the _Secretum,_ he gave it the form of a dialogue between Augustine and the author, and it is Augustine who takes the part of the spiritual guide who resolves the doubts and questions of the poet. And in the famous letter describing his climbing of Mont Ventoux, Petrarch tells us that he took Augustine's _Confessions_ out of his pocket, opened them at random, and found a passage which appropriately expressed his own feelings: "Men go to admire the heights of the mountains, the great floods of the sea, the shores of the ocean, and the orbits of the stars, and neglect themselves." Thus it was the Augustine of the _Confessions,_ the man who eloquently expresses his feelings and experiences, not the dogmatic theologian, who impressed Petrarch and other later humanists and helped them to reconcile their religious convictions with their literary tastes and personal opinions. Only Erasmus, who had done so much for the text of Augustine, was unsympathetic to his theology and to his interpretation of the Bible, preferring that of St. Jerome, and significantly enough was taken to task for it by Catholics and Protestants alike.

Another strand of Augustinian influence in the Renaissance may be found among the Platonists of the period. Augustine's witness in favor of Plato and the Platonists, already utilized by Petrarch against the authority of Aristotle, was eagerly cited by all philosophers sympathetic to Platonism from Bessarion to Patrizi. At least some of these Platonists also derived important philosophical ideas from the writings of Augustine. Thus Cusanus, who was in many ways affected by the thought of Augustine, took from one of his letters the term "learned ignorance," which he used to describe the characteristic method of his speculation. And Ficino not only states that his allegiance to the Platonic school was partly determined by the authority of Augustine, but also derived from a direct reading of Augustine's works some very essential elements of his philosophy, as a more detailed analysis of his works would easily show. To mention only one example, when Ficino in the preface to his main philosophical work announces his intention of interpreting Plato's philosophy primarily in terms of the soul and of God, he is clearly following the lead of St. Augustine. Yet it is again characteristic that Ficino seems to know Augustine mainly from such well-known works as the *Confessions,* the *City of God,* and the *De Trinitate,* and in addition from those early philosophical and Platonist writings that have been minimized by the theological admirers of the great Church Father, whereas he apparently showed less interest in Augustine's later theological writings.

Very different but no less powerful was the influence which Augustine exercised upon the theological writers, both Protestant and Catholic, of the sixteenth and seventeenth centuries. It was the theology of the later writings of Augustine, with their emphasis on predestination, sin, and grace, which was taken up by Luther and Calvin and their successors, whereas the theologians of the Catholic Reformation, and later the Jansenists and Oratorians, derived very different theological ideas from the interpretation of Augustine's thought. It is true that these theological developments were far removed from the interests and ideas of Renaissance humanism, but it seems reasonable to remember that the authority granted to Augustine, to the other patristic writers, and to Scripture itself has something to do with the humanist emphasis on ancient sources and with their contempt for the medieval tradition of scholastic theology.

I think we are now at last prepared to offer a meaningful interpretation of the term "Christian humanism" that is so often applied to the Renaissance or to earlier periods.[30] Confining the term humanism, according to the Renaissance meaning of the words humanist and humanities, to the rhetorical, classical, and moral concerns of the Renaissance humanists, regardless of the particular philosophical or theological opinions held by individual humanists, and of the theological, philosophical, scientific, or juristic training which individual scholars may have combined with their humanist education, we might choose to call Christian humanists all those scholars who accepted the teachings of Christianity and were members of one of the churches, without necessarily discussing religious or theological topics in their literary or scholarly writings. By this standard, practically all Renaissance humanists, before and after the Reformation, were Christian humanists, since the alleged cases of openly pagan or atheistic convictions are rare and dubious. But it is probably preferable to use the term Christian humanism in a more specific sense, and to limit it to those scholars with a humanist classical and rhetorical training who explicitly discussed religious or theological problems in all or some of their writings. In this sense, neither Aquinas nor Luther were Christian humanists, for the simple reason that they were theologians, but not humanists as that term was then understood, although Luther presupposes certain scholarly achievements of humanism. On the other hand, we must list among the Christian humanists not only Erasmus, Vives, Budé, and More, but also Calvin, the elegant Latin writer and commentator of Seneca; Melanchthon, the defender of rhetoric against philosophy, who had more influence on many aspects of Lutheran Germany than Luther himself and who was responsible for the humanistic tradition of the German Protestant schools down to the nineteenth century; and finally the Jesuit Fathers, many of whom were excellent classical scholars and Latin writers, and who owed part of their success to the good instruction offered in their schools and colleges in the then fashionable humanistic disciplines. For the tradition of humanist learning by no means came to an end with the Protestant or Catholic Reformations, as might appear if we look only for the headlines of the historical development. It survived as vigorously as did the tradition of Aristotelian scholasticism, cutting across all religious and national divisions, flourishing at Leiden and Oxford no less than at Padua and Salamanca, and exercising as formative an influence upon the minds of the philosophers and scientists trained in the schools and universities of the seventeenth and eighteenth centuries.

We have at last reached the end of our long and rapid journey, and it is time for me to thank you for having kept me company, and to sum up my impressions and recollections. We might state briefly that the period which we call the Renaissance attained a much more accurate and more complete acquaintance with ancient Latin and especially Greek literature than had been possible in the preceding age. And we have tried to show with a few examples taken from the history of philosophy and theology that this acquaintance was not merely a matter of study and of imitation, but that the ideas embodied in ancient literature served as a ferment and inspiration for the original thought of the period, and account at least in part for the intellectual changes which occurred more slowly in the fifteenth and more rapidly in the sixteenth centuries. These examples could easily be multiplied from the history of philosophy as well as from all other areas of intellectual and cultural history.

With the seventeenth century, there begins a new period in the history of Western science and philosophy, and the traditions of the Renaissance begin to recede into the background. Beginning about the middle of the sixteenth century, scholars started to be more conscious of their originality, and to notice the progress made by their own time in comparison with classical antiquity.[31] The invention of printing and the discovery of America were now emphasized to illustrate this progress, and during the seventeenth century, the famous battle of the ancients and moderns led to a clearer distinction between the sciences, in which modern times had by now surpassed the achievements of the ancients, and the arts, in which the ancients could never be surpassed though perhaps equaled. Consequently, when a new wave of classicism arose during the eighteenth century, it was limited to literature and poetry and to the visual arts, but omitted the natural sciences in which the ancients could no longer be considered as masters.

We are now living in a time in which this wave of eighteenth-century classicism has nearly spent its force. Classical scholarship has become a highly specialized tool in the hands of a few brave experts who have greatly expanded the knowledge of their predecessors, at least in certain areas of their discipline, but who have seemed to lose, through no fault of their own, more and more ground with the nonspecialists and with the people at large. Those who are not trained classical philologists now have reason to envy any medieval century for at least its Latin learning, and there are many professional educators and many important sectors of public opinion that seem to be completely unaware of the existence, let alone the importance, of humanistic scholarship. The situation is such that many responsible scholars are rightly worried. Yet I am inclined to hope and to expect that the interest in the classics and in historical learning will be continued and even revived, for I am firmly convinced of their intrinsic merit, and believe that it cannot fail to impose itself again, although perhaps in a form different from the one to which we are accustomed, and more in accordance with the needs and interests of our time and society. Thus the study of the history of civilization and the reading of the classical authors in translations perform a useful service in college education. The wheel of fashion which in modern times seems to have replaced the wheel of fortune that appears so frequently in the art and literature of the Middle Ages and of the Renaissance, is likely to bring back at some time that taste for clarity, simplicity, and conciseness in literature and in thought that has always found its nourishment in the works of antiquity. The natural desire to overcome the limits of our parochial outlook in time as well as in place may stimulate the interest in the classics; for they have not only a direct appeal for our own time, but also hold many clues for the understanding of medieval and early modern thought, which contains in turn the direct roots of our own contemporary world. It is true that each generation has its own message, and each individual may make his own original contribution. The effect of the classics upon Renaissance thought and literature may show us that it is possible to learn from the past and to be original at the same time. Originality is greatly to be admired, but it is a gift of nature or providence; it cannot be taught, and I doubt that it is harmed by knowledge or increased by ignorance.

I do not wish to give the impression that I want to elevate the ideal of scholarship at the expense of other more fundamental and more comprehensive ideals, or that I ignore the limitations of historical learning. We all are, or want to be, not merely scholars, but citizens, persons who work, persons who think, if not philosophers, and human beings. Historical knowledge, as Jacob Burckhardt said, does not make us shrewder for the next time, but wiser forever.[32] It gives us perspective, but it does not give us answers or solutions to the moral, social, or intellectual problems which we face. No amount of information will relieve us of the choices in judgment and in action which we are compelled to make every day. There are unique feelings and experiences in every person's external and spiritual life that have never, or rarely and imperfectly, been expressed by the thinkers and writers of the past. The world of Western civilization, wide and rich in comparison with our present time and society which is but a part of it, is itself small and limited when compared with the entire history of mankind, with the existence of animals, of plants, and of silent nature on our planet, or with the huge, if not infinite, extent in space and time of our visible universe. Exclusive concern for historical scholarship may isolate us from all those persons who for geographical, social or educational reasons cannot participate in it and who as human beings yet demand our sympathetic understanding. Finally, the record of the past in which all battles are decided and many pains forgotten, whereas the most distinguished characters, actions, and works stand out more clearly and in a more final form than they did in their own time, may lull us into a false security and indolence in view of the pains we have to suffer, the decisions we have to make, the actions and works we have to accomplish, without yet knowing the outcome, or the value they may have if and when they appear in turn as a settled and hardened past to a future observer. All these objections and doubts are true, and should be always remembered. Nevertheless, I hope you will accept with patience this plea for classical scholarship and historical knowledge, since it comes from a person who is not a member of the guild of philologists or historians, and allow me to conclude with a word of Erasmus which he gave as a reply to those theologians who criticized his ideal of scholarship, and which we might easily adapt to our somewhat different situation: "Prayer, to be sure, is the stronger weapon (in our fight against vice) . . . yet knowledge is no less necessary."[88]

GENERAL BIBLIOGRAPHY

BOLGAR, R. R. *The Classical Heritage and Its Beneficiaries.* Cambridge, 1954.

CASSIRER, E. *Das Erkenntnisproblem.* vol. I. Berlin, 1922.

———— *Individuum und Kosmos in der Philosophie der Renaissance.* Berlin-Leipzig, 1927.

CASSIRER, E., P. O. KRISTELLER, AND J. H. RANDALL, eds. *The Renaissance Philosophy of Man.* Chicago, 1948.

CURTIUS, E. R. *Europäische Literatur und lateinisches Mittelalter.* Bern, 1948.

DE WULF, M. *Histoire de la philosophie médiévale.* 6th ed. 3 vols. Louvain, 1934-1947.

DUHEM, P. *Etudes sur Léonard de Vinci.* 3 vols. Paris 1906-1913.

GARIN, E. *La filosofia.* 2 vols. Milan, 1947.

———— *Der italienische Humanismus.* Bern, 1947.

GENTILE, G. *La filosofia.* Milan, 1904-1915.

GILSON, E. *La philosophie au moyen âge.* 3rd ed. Paris, 1947.

GRABMANN, M. *Mittelalterliches Geistesleben.* 2 vols. Munich, 1926-1936.

———— *Die Geschichte der scholastischen Methode.* 2 vols. Freiburg, 1909-1911.

HASKINS, CHARLES H. *Studies in Mediaeval Culture.* Oxford, 1929.

———— *Studies in the History of Mediaeval Science.* 2nd ed. Cambridge, Mass., 1927.

HIGHET, G. *The Classical Tradition.* Oxford, 1949.

KRISTELLER, P. O., AND J. H. RANDALL. "The Study of the Philosophies of the Renaissance," *Journal of the History of Ideas,* II (1941), 449-496.

MANITIUS, M. *Geschichte der lateinischen Literatur des Mittelalters.* 3 vols. Munich, 1911-1931.

MARROU, H.-I. *Histoire de l'éducation dans l'antiquité.* Paris, 1948.

OLSCHKI, L. *Geschichte der neusprachlichen wissenschaftlichen Literatur.* 3 vols. Heidelberg, 1919 — Halle, 1927.

PARÉ, G., and others. *La Renaissance du XIIe siècle.* Paris-Ottawa, 1933.

RASHDALL, H. *The Universities of Europe in the Middle Ages.* New ed. by F. M. Powicke and A. B. Emden. 3 vols. Oxford, 1936.

RENUCCI, P. *L'Aventure de l'Humanisme Européen au Moyen Age.* Paris, 1953.

SABBADINI, R. *Le scoperte dei codici latini e greci ne' secoli XIV e XV.* 2 vols. Florence, 1905-1914.

SAITTA, G. *Il pensiero italiano nell' umanesimo e nel rinascimento.* 3 vols. Bologna, 1949-1951.

SANDYS, SIR J. E. *A History of Classical Scholarship.* 3 vols. Cambridge, 1908-1921.

SARTON, G. *Introduction to the History of Science.* 3 vols. Baltimore, 1927-1948.

Storia letteraria d'Italia. Milan: Vallardi. Many vols., especially, V. Rossi, *Il Quattrocento,* 1933.

THORNDIKE, L. *A History of Magic and Experimental Science.* 6 vols. New York, 1923-1941.

TIRABOSCHI, G, *Storia della letteratura italiana.* 25 in 14 vols. Venice, 1823.

TOFFANIN, G. *Storia dell' umanesimo.* 3 vols. Bologna, 1950.

UEBERWEG, F. *Grundriss der Geschichte der Philosophie.* vols. I-III. Berlin, 1924-1928.

VOIGT, G. *Die Wiederbelebung des classischen Althertums.* 3rd ed. 2 vols. Berlin, 1893.

WOODWARD, WILLIAM H. *Studies in Education during the Age of the Renaissance.* Cambridge, 1906.

———— *Vittorino da Feltre and other Humanist Educators.* Cambridge, 1905.

ZELLER, E. *Die Philosophie der Griechen.* 3 vols. in 6. Leipzig, 1919-1923.

NOTES

1. THE HUMANIST MOVEMENT

1. J. Burckhardt, *Die Cultur der Renaissance in Italian* (Basel, 1860); J. A. Symonds, *Renaissance in Italy*, 7 vols. (London, 1875-1886); J. Huizinga, *The Waning of the Middle Ages* (London, 1924); Wallace K. Ferguson, *The Renaissance in Historical Thought* (Boston, 1948); E. Panofsky, "Renaissance and Renascences." *Kenyon Review*, VI (1944), 201-236; discussion on the Renaissance by D. Durand, H. Baron, and others, in *Journal of the History of Ideas*, IV (1943), 1-74; P. O. Kristeller, "Humanism and Scholasticism in the Italian Renaissance," *Byzantion*, XVII (1944-1945), 346-374.

2. *The Battle of the Seven Arts . . . by Henri d'Andeli*, ed. L. J. Paetow (Berkeley, 1914); E. Norden, *Die antike Kunstprosa*, II (Leipzig, 1898), 688ff and 724ff.

3. For some distinguished examples, see: E. Gilson, *Saint Thomas d'Aquin* (Paris, 1925), 6-7; The same, "Humanisme médiéval et Renaissance," in his *Les Idées et les Lettres* (Paris, 1932), 189ff; Douglas Bush, *The Renaissance and English Humanism* (Toronto, 1939), 48ff; The same, *Classical Influences in Renaissance Literature* (Cambridge, Mass., 1952) 48ff; Gerald G. Walsh, *Medieval Humanism* (New York, 1942), 1: "Humanism, in general, I take to be the idea that a human being is meant to achieve, during life, a fair measure of human happiness" (by that definition, Aristotle is a humanist, but Petrarch is not); Renucci, *L' Aventure de l'Humanisme Européen au Moyen Age* (Paris, 1953), 9.

4. W. Rüegg, *Cicero und der Humanismus* (Zurich, 1946), 1ff.

5. Kristeller, "Humanism and Scholasticism," 365-367; A. Campana, "The Origin of the Word 'Humanist,'" *Journal of the Warburg and Courtauld Institutes*, IX (1946), 60-73.

6. W. Jaeger, *Humanism and Theology* (Milwaukee, 1943), 20ff, 72ff; R. Pfeiffer, *Humanitas Erasmiana* (Leipzig-Berlin, 1931).

7. Kristeller, "Humanism and Scholasticism."

8. As has been done, to a certain extent, by E. Garin (*Der italienische Humanismus*, Bern, 1947).

9. H. von Arnim, *Leben und Werke des Dio von Prusa* (Berlin, 1898), 4-114; H. Gomperz, *Sophistik und Rhetorik* (Leipzig, 1912); W. Jaeger, *Paideia*, I (Oxford, 1939, chapter on the Sophists) and III (1944, chapters on Isocrates).

10. R. McKeon, "Rhetoric in the Middle Ages," *Speculum*, XVII (1942), 1-32.

11. A Galletti, *L'Eloquenza* (Milan, 1904-1938).

12. R. Sabbadini, *Le scoperte dei codici latini e greci ne' secoli XIV e XV*, 2 vols. (Florence, 1905-1914). Cf. M. Manitius, *Handschriften antiker Autoren in mittelalterlichen Bibliothekskatalogen* (Leipzig, 1935); G. Billanovich, "Pet-

rarch and the Textual Tradition of Livy," *Journal of the Warburg and Court-auld Institutes,* XIV (1951), 137-208.

13.   Louise R. Loomis, *Medieval Hellenism* (Lancaster, Pa. 1906). Valuable recent studies by R. Weiss and others do not fundamentally alter this picture.

14.   K. Krumbacher, *Geschichte der byzantinischen Literatur,* 2nd ed. (Munich, 1897) ; L. Bréhier, *La civilisation byzantine* (Paris, 1950) ; A. A. Vasiliev, *History of the Byzantine Empire* (Madison, Wis., 1952), 713-722 ; J. Verpeaux, "Byzance et l'humanisme," *Bulletin de l'Association Guillaume Budé,* ser. 3, no. 3 (October 1952), 25-38.

15.   M. De Wulf, *Histoire de la philosophie médiévale* (Louvain, 1934-1947), I (1934), 64-80, II (1936), 25-58 (these valuable sections by A. Pelzer have not been completely included in the American translation) ; G. Sarton, *Introduction to the History of Science,* 3 vols. (Baltimore, 1927-1948) ; J. T. Muckle, "Greek Works translated directly into Latin before 1350," *Mediaeval Studies,* IV (1942), 33-42, V (1943), 102-114; G. Lacombe and others, *Aristoteles Latinus,* I (Rome, 1939) ; E. Garin, "Le traduzioni umanistiche di Aristotele nel secolo XV," *Atti dell 'Accademia Fiorentina di Scienze Morali 'La Colombaria',* VIII (1950).

16.   Cf. the works of Gentile, Saitta, and Garin.

17.   C. Lenient, *De Ciceroniano bello apud recentiores* (Paris, 1855) ; R. Sabbadini, *Storia del Ciceronianismo* (Turin, 1885) ; Th. Zielinski, *Cicero im Wandel der Jahrhunderte,* 3rd ed. (Leipzig, 1912) ; H. Baron, "Cicero and the Roman Civic Spirit in the Middle Ages and Early Renaissance," *Bulletin of the John Rylands Library,* XXII (1938), 72-97; W. Rüegg, *Cicero und der Humanismus;* Izora Scott, *Controversies over the Imitation of Cicero* (New York, 1910).

18.   Alamanno Rinuccini, *Lettere ed Orazioni,* ed. V. R. Giustiniani (Florence, 1953), 97.

19.   P. O. Kristeller, "Florentine Platonism and Its Relations with Humanism and Scholasticism," *Church History,* VIII (1939), 201-211.

20.   G. Gentile, "Il concetto dell'uomo nel Rinascimento," in his *Il Pensiero italiano del Rinascimento,* 3rd ed. (Florence, 1940), 47-113; P. O. Kristeller, "The Philosophy of Man in the Italian Renaissance," *Italica,* XXIV (1947), 93-112.

21.   Cf. "Du repentir," *Essais,* III, 2.

2.   THE ARISTOTELIAN TRADITION

1.   W. Jaeger, *Aristotle,* 2nd ed. (Oxford, 1948).

2.   Cf. R. Klibansky, *The Continuity of the Platonic Tradition during the Middle Ages* (Oxford, 1939), 13.

3.   B. Tatakis, *La philosophie byzantine* (E. Bréhier, *Histoire de la philosophie,* deuxième fascicule supplémentaire, Paris, 1949). See above, ch. 1, n. 14.

4.   M. Steinschneider, *Die Arabischen Uebersetzungen aus dem Griechischen (Beihefte zum Centralblatt für Bibliothekswesen,* no. 5, Leipzig, 1890, 51-82; no. 12, 1893, 129-240) ; R. Walzer, "Arabic Transmission of Greek Thought to Medieval Europe," *Bulletin of the John Rylands Library,* XXIX (1945-1946), 160-183.

5. See ch. 1, n. 15. M. Steinschneider, "Die europäischen Übersetzungen aus dem Arabischen," *Sitzungsberichte der Kaiserlichen Akademie der Wissenschaften in Wien, Philosophisch-Historische Klasse,* vol. 149 (1904), no. 4, vol. 151 (1906), no. 1.

6. H. Rashdall, *The Universities of Europe in the Middle Ages* (Oxford, 1936); H. Denifle and E. Chatelain, *Chartularium Universitatis Parisiensis,* 4 vols. (Paris, 1889-1897).

7. For some curious examples, see E. A. Moody, "Galileo and Avempace," *Journal of the History of Ideas,* XII (1951), 163-193, 375-422.

8. E. Renan, *Averroès et l'averroïsme,* 3rd ed. (Paris, 1867); P. Mandonnet, *Siger de Brabant et l'averroïsme latin au XIII e siècle,* 2nd ed. (Louvain, 1908-1911); F. Van Steenberghen, *Les œuvres et la doctrine de Siger de Brabant* (Brussels, 1938); The same, *Siger de Brabant d'après ses oeuvres inédites,* 2 vols. (Louvain, 1931-1942); B. Nardi, *Sigieri di Brabante nel pensiero del Rinascimento italiano* (Rome, 1945); The same, "Averroismo," *Enciclopedia Cattolica,* II (Vatican City, 1949), 524-530; Anneliese Maier, "Eine italienische Averroistenschule aus der ersten Hälfte des 14. Jahrhunderts," in her *Die Vorläufer Galileis im 14. Jahrhundert* (Rome, 1949), 251-278; P. O. Kristeller, "Petrarch's 'Averroists,'" *Bibliothèque d'Humanisme et Renaissance,* XIV (1952), 59-65.

9. Ricardo G. Villoslada, *La Universidad de Paris durante los estudios de Francisco de Vitoria* (Rome, 1938).

10. C. Giacon, *La seconda scolastica,* 3 vols. (Milan, 1944-1950).

11. P. Petersen, *Geschichte der Aristotelischen Philosophie im protestantischen Deutschland* (Leipzig, 1921); M. Wundt, *Die deutsche Schulmetaphysik des 17. Jahrhunderts* (Tübingen, 1939).

12. E. Gilson, *Etudes sur le rôle de la pensée médiévale dans la formation du système cartésien* (Paris, 1930); Matthias Meier, *Descartes und die Renaissance* (Münster, 1914); L. Blanchet, *Les antécédents historiques du 'Je pense, donc je suis,'* (Paris, 1920); H. A. Wolfson, *The Philosophy of Spinoza,* 2 vols. (Cambridge, Mass., 1934); J. Politella, *Platonism, Aristotelianism and Cabalism in the Philosophy of Leibniz* (Philadelphia, 1938).

13. Grabmann, *Mittelalterliches Geistesleben,* II (1936), 239-271; The same, "Gentile da Cingoli," *Sitzungsberichte der Bayerischen Akademie der Wissenschaften, Philosophisch-Historische Abteilung,* Jahrgang 1940 (Munich, 1941), no. 9; The same, "L'Aristotelismo italiano al tempo di Dante," *Rivista di filosofia neo-scolastica,* XXXVIII (1946), 260-277; B. Nardi, "L'averroismo bolognese nel secolo XIII e Taddeo Alderotto," *Rivista di storia della filosofia,* XXIII (1931), 504-517. Cf. n. 8 above.

14. M. Clagett, *Giovanni Marliani and late medieval physics* (New York, 1941).

15. J. H. Randall, Jr., "The Development of Scientific Method in the School of Padua," *Journal of the History of Ideas,* I (1940), 177-206; E. Cassirer, *Das Erkenntnisproblem,* I (1922), 117ff.

16. F. Ehrle, *Der Sentenzenkommentar Peters von Candia* (Münster, 1925), 114ff; Villoslada, *La Universidad de Paris,* 279-307.

17. P. O. Kristeller, "Un codice padovano di Aristotele postillato da Francesco e Ermolao Barbaro," *Bibliofilia*, L (1948), 162-178; E. Garin, "Le traduzioni umanistiche di Aristotele."

18. In Francesco Patrizi's *Discussiones Peripateticae* (Basel, 1581).

19. This is quite apparent both from the manuscripts and from the commentaries.

20. Aristotle, *De arte poetica Guillelmo de Moerbeke interprete*, ed E. Valgimigli, E. Franceschini, and L. Minio-Paluello (*Aristoteles Latinus*, vol. XXXIII, Bruges-Paris, 1953).

21. J. E. Spingarn, *A History of Literary Criticism in the Renaissance*, 2nd ed. (New York, 1908); G. Toffanin, *La fine dell'umanesimo* (Turin, 1920).

22. For example, in the work of Ulisse Aldrovandi.

23. L. Zanta, *La renaissance du stoïcisme au XVI e siècle* (Paris, 1914); P. O. Kristeller, "Ficino and Pomponazzi on the Place of Man in the Universe," *Journal of the History of Ideas*, V (1944), 220-226; The same, "A New Manuscript Source for Pomponazzi's Theory of the Soul. . . ," *Revue Internationale de Philosophie*, vol. II, fasc. 2 (16 of series) (1951), 144-157; J. H. Randall in *The Renaissance Philosophy of Man* (Chicago, 1948), 257-279.

24. E. Garin, *Prosatori latini del Quattrocento* (Milan, 1952), 41ff (for Bruni); Q. Breen, "Giovanni Pico della Mirandola on the Conflict of Philosophy and Rhetoric. . . . ," *Journal of the History of Ideas*, XIII (1952), 384-426 (for Ermolao).

25. Paetow, ed., *The Battle of the Seven Arts;* L. Thorndike, *Science and Thought in the Fifteenth Century* (New York, 1929), 24-58; E. Garin, *La disputa delle arti nel Quattrocento* (Florence, 1947).

26. Perry Miller, *The New England Mind* (New York, 1939).

27. In his *De tradendis disciplinis*.

28. P. O. Kristeller, "Florentine Platonism"; The same, "The Scholastic Background of Marsilio Ficino," *Traditio*, II (1944), 257ff; E. Garin, *Giovanni Pico della Mirandola* (Florence, 1937); Avery Dulles, *Princeps Concordiae* (Cambridge, Mass., 1941); Q. Breen, "Giovanni Pico della Mirandola."

29. Cassirer, *Erkenntnisproblem*, I (1922).

30. Edward W. Strong, *Procedures and Metaphysics* (Berkeley, 1936).

31. Moody, "Galileo and Avempace."

32. A. Koyré, *Etudes Galiléennes*, 3 vols. (Paris, 1939).

3. RENAISSANCE PLATONISM

1. Alfred N. Whitehead, *Process and Reality* (New York, 1941), 63.

2. P. Merlan, *From Platonism to Neoplatonism* (The Hague, 1953).

3. H. Cherniss, *The Riddle of the Early Academy* (Berkeley, 1945).

4. W. Theiler, *Die Vorbereitung des Neuplatonismus* (Berlin, 1930).

5. J. Festugière, *La révélation d' Hermès Trismegiste*, 4 vols. (Paris, 1944-1954).

6. Proclus, *The Elements of Theology*, ed. and tr. E. R. Dodds (Oxford, 1933).

7. R. Klibansky, *The Continuity of the Platonic Tradition during the Middle Ages* (London, 1939 and 1950). This little book is the most important single, though not the only, source of this lecture down to the fifteenth century. Cf. also P. Shorey, *Platonism Ancient and Modern* (Berkeley, 1938).

8. See ch. 1, n. 14, and ch. 2, n. 3.

9. Milton V. Anastos, "Pletho's Calendar and Liturgy," *Dumbarton Oaks Papers* IV (1948), 183-305.

10. L. Mohler, *Kardinal Bessarion*, 3 vols. (Paderborn, 1923-1942).

11. See ch. 2, n. 4. F. Rosenthal, "On the Knowledge of Plato's Philosophy in the Islamic World," *Islamic Culture*, XIV (1940), 387-422.

12. G. Scholem, *Major Trends in Jewish Mysticism* (Jerusalem, 1941).

13. *De Civitate Dei*, VIII, 5 and 9ff, IX, 1, X, 1; P. Courcelle, *Recherches sur les Confessions de Saint Augustin* (Paris, 1950).

14. G. Théry, *Etudes Dionysiennes* (Paris, 1932-1937).

15. Toni Schmid, "Ein Timaioskommentar in Sigtuna," *Classica et Mediaevalia*, X (1948), 220-266.

16. E. Garin, "Una fonte ermetica poco nota," *La Rinascita*, vol. III, fasc. 12 (1940), 202-232.

17. Corpus Platonicum Medii Aevi: *Meno interprete Henrico Aristippo*, ed. V. Kordeuter and C. Labowsky (London, 1940); *Phaedo interprete Henrico Aristippo*, ed. L. Minio-Paluello (London, 1950); *Parmenides . . . nec non Procli Commentarium in Parmenidem, pars ultima adhuc inedita interprete Guillelmo de Moerbeka*, ed. R. Klibansky and C. Labowsky (London, 1953).

18. A. Hyma, *The Christian Renaissance* (Grand Rapids, 1924).

19. Mohler, *Kardinal Bessarion*.

20. G. Gentile, "Le traduzioni medievali di Platone e Francesco Petrarca," in his *Studi sul Rinascimento*, 2nd ed. (Florence, 1936), 23-88; L. Minio-Paluello, "Il Fedone latino con note autografe del Petrarca," *Accademia Nazionale dei Lincei, Rendiconti della Classe di Scienze morali, storiche e filologiche*, ser. VIII, vol. IV (1949), 107-113.

21. For a list of humanist versions of Plato, see P. O. Kristeller, *Supplementum Ficinianum*, I (Florence, 1937), p. clvi-clvii. For the versions of Bruni, see Leonardo Bruni Aretino, *Humanistisch-Philosophische Schriften*, ed. H. Baron (Leipzig-Berlin, 1928), 161, 163, 172-174; L. Bertalot, "Zur Bibliographie der Übersetzungen des Leonardus Brunus Aretinus," *Quellen und Forschungen aus italienischen Archiven und Bibliotheken*, XXVII (1937), 180-184. For Trapezuntius' version of the *Parmenides*, see R. Klibansky, "Plato's Parmenides in the Middle Ages and the Renaissance," *Mediaeval and Renaissance Studies*, vol. I, pt. 2 (1943) 289-304.

22. E. Vansteenberghe, *Le Cardinal Nicolas de Cues* (Paris, 1920).

23. P. O. Kristeller, *The Philosophy of Marsilio Ficino* (New York, 1943); *Il pensiero filosofico di Marsilio Ficino* (Florence, 1953); G. Saitta, *Marsilio Ficino e la filosofia dell'umanesimo*, 3rd ed. (Bologna, 1954).

24. E. Garin, *Giovanni Pico della Mirandola* (Florence, 1937); E. Anagnine, *G. Pico della Mirandola* (Bari, 1937).

25. Ioannes Picus, *Oratio de hominis dignitate,* in Latin and English (Lexington, Ky., 1953).

26. P. O. Kristeller, "Francesco da Diacceto and Florentine Platonism in the Sixteenth Century," *Miscellanea Giovanni Mercati,* IV (Vatican City, 1946), 260-304; Nesca A. Robb, *Neoplatonism of the Italian Renaissance* (London, 1935).

27. S. Greenberg, *The Infinite in Giordano Bruno* (New York, 1950); Dorothy W. Singer, *Giordano Bruno* (New York, 1950).

28. R. Marcel, "Les 'découvertes' d'Erasme en Angleterre," *Bibliothèque d'Humanisme et Renaissance,* XIV (1952) 117-123.

29. J. Hexter, *More's Utopia* (Princeton, 1952).

30. A. Renaudet, *Préréforme et Humanisme à Paris* (Paris, 1916).

31. Chr. Sigwart, *Ulrich Zwingli, Der Charakter seiner Theologie mit besonderer Rücksicht auf Picus von Mirandola dargestellt* (Stuttgart, 1855).

32. J. Blau, *The Christian Interpretation of the Cabala in the Renaissance* (New York, 1944).

33. Roy W. Battenhouse, "The Doctrine of Man in Calvin and in Renaissance Platonism," *Journal of the History of Ideas,* IX (1948), 447-471.

34. E. Massa, "L'anima e l'uomo in Egidio di Viterbo e nelle fonte classiche e medievali," *Testi Umanistici inediti sul 'De Anima'* (*Archivio di Filosofia,* Padua, 1951), 37-86.

35. J. D. Mansi, *Sacrorum Conciliorum Nova et Amplissima Collectio,* XXXII (Paris, 1902), 842-843.

36. W. Moench, *Die italienische Platonrenaissance und ihre Bedeutung für Frankreichs Literatur- und Geistesgeschichte* (Berlin, 1936).

37. Sears Jayne, "Ficino and the Platonism of the English Renaissance," *Comparative Literature,* IV (1952), 214-238.

38. Robb, *Neoplatonism of the Italian Renaissance,* 177ff; L. Tonelli, *L'amore nella poesia e nel pensiero del Rinascimento* (Florence, 1933).

39. In his *Poetica,* a work of which I was able to discover extensive unpublished sections in a group of manuscripts (Parma, Biblioteca Palatina, cod. Pal. 408, 417, and 421).

40. P. O. Kristeller, "The Modern System of the Arts," *Journal of the History of Ideas,* XII (1951), 496-527, XIII (1952), 17-46.

41. E. Panosfky, *Idea* (Leipzig-Berlin, 1924).

42. E. H. Gombrich, "Botticelli's Mythologies," *Journal of the Warburg and Courtauld Institutes,* VIII (1945), 7-60; D. Redig de Campos, "Il concetto platonico-cristiano della Stanza della Segnatura," in his *Raffaello e Michelangelo* (Rome, 1946), 9-27; E. Panofsky, *Studies in Iconology* (New York, 1939), 171ff.

43. O. Kinkeldey, "Franchino Gafori and Marsilio Ficino," *Harvard Library Bulletin,* I (1947), 379-382; P. O. Kristeller, "Music and Learning in the Early Italian Renaissance," *Journal of Renaissance and Baroque Music,* I (1947), 255-274.

44. Leonardo da Vinci's attitude towards humanism and Platonism has been a subject of controversy. For a more positive opinion, see now: A. Chastel, "Léonard et la culture," in *Léonard de Vinci et l'expérience scientifique au seizième siècle* (Paris, 1953), 251-263.

45. E. Cassirer, *Das Erkenntnisproblem* (Berlin, 1922); E. A. Burtt, *The Metaphysical Foundations of Modern Physical Science* (New York, 1951).

46. B. Brickman, *An Introduction to Francesco Patrizi's Nova de Universis Philosophia* (New York, 1941).

47. Randall, "The Development of Scientific Method"; Moody, "Galileo and Avempace"; A. Koyré, "Galileo and Plato," *Journal of the History of Ideas,* IV (1943), 400-428; E. Cassirer, "Galileo's Platonism," *Studies and Essays in the History of Science and Learning in Honor of George Sarton* (New York, 1946), 279-297.

48. ". . . quando uno non sa la verità da per sè, è impossibile che altri glie ne faccia sapere . . . le vere (cose), cioè le necessarie, cioè quelle che è impossibile ad esser altrimenti, ogni mediocre discorso o le sa da sè o è impossible che ei le sappia mai . . ." *Dialogo sopra i due massimi sistemi del mondo, Seconda giornata,* in Galileo Galilei, *Le Opere,* VII (Florence, 1933), 183; Galileo Galilei, *Dialogue concerning the two chief world systems,* tr. S. Drake (Berkeley, 1953), 157-158; Galileo Galilei, *Dialogue on the Great World Systems,* tr. T. Salusbury, ed. G. de Santillana (Chicago, 1953), 172.

49. See ch. 2, n. 12.

50. E. Cassirer, *Die platonische Renaissance in England und die Schule von Cambridge* (Leipzig, 1932); *The Platonic Renaissance in England,* tr. J. P. Pettegrove (Austin, Tex., 1953).

4. PAGANISM AND CHRISTIANITY

1. Similar views on the Renaissance are still expressed by R. Niebuhr, *The Nature and Destiny of Man,* I (New York, 1941), 61ff, II (1943), 157ff.

2. J.-R. Charbonnel, *La pensée italienne au XVI e siècle et le courant libertin* (Paris, 1919).

3. P. O. Kristeller, "El Mito del Ateísmo Renacentista y la tradición francesa del librepensamiento," *Notas y Estudios de Filosofía,* vol. IV, fasc. 13 (1953), 1-14.

4. E. Walser, *Gesammelte Studien zur Geistesgeschichte der Renaissance* (Basel, 1952), especially 48-63: "Christentum und Antike in der Auffassung der italienischen Frührenaissance," and 96-128: "Studien zur Weltanschauung der Renaissance."

5. The term Pantheist was coined by John Toland in 1705 (*The Oxford English Dictionary,* VII [Oxford, 1933], 430).

6. Charbonnel, *La pensée italienne.*

7. A. Hyma, *The Christian Renaissance* (Grand Rapids, 1924).

8. This point is duly emphasized by Burckhardt (Part VI, ch. 2).

9. G. M. Monti, *Le confraternite medievali dell'alta e media Italia,* 2 vols. (Venice, 1927).

10. Wallace K. Ferguson in a lecture.

11. K. Burdach, *Reformation, Renaissance, Humanismus,* 2nd ed. (Berlin-Leipzig, 1926).

12. G. Toffanin, *Storia dell 'umanesimo; Che cosa fu l'umanesimo* (Florence, 1929).

13. H.-I. Marrou, *Saint Augustin et la fin de la culture antique* (Paris, 1938) ; Renucci, *L'Aventure de l'Humanisme Européen au Moyen Age;* Martin R. P. McGuire, "Mediaeval Humanism," *The Catholic Historical Review,* XXXVIII (1953), 397-409.

14. Charles N. Cochrane, *Christianity and Classical Culture* (London, 1944), cf. my review in the *Journal of Philosophy,* XLI (1944), 576-581; Harry A. Wolfson, *Philo,* 2 vols. (Cambridge, Mass., 1947), cf. my review in the *Journal of Philosophy,* XLVI (1949), 359-363. One may also compare the manner in which E. Gilson (*Les Métamorphoses de la cité de Dieu* [Louvain-Paris, 1952], 6ff) tries to evade the obvious contribution of Stoicism to the notion of human solidarity.

15. M. Grabmann, *Die Geschichte der katholischen Theologie* (Freiburg, 1933), 15ff; J. De Ghellinck, *Le mouvement théologique du XII e siècle,* 2nd ed. (Brussels-Paris, 1948) ; Artur M. Landgraf, *Einführung in die Geschichte der theologischen Literatur der Frühscholastik* (Regensburg, 1948).

16. P. O. Kristeller, "Augustine and the Early Renaissance," *Review of Religion,* VIII (1944), 339-358.

17. P. De Nolhac, *Pétrarque et l'humanisme,* 2nd ed. (Paris, 1907).

18. Q. Breen, *John Calvin: A Study in French Humanism* (Grand Rapids, 1931) ; Paul Wernle, *Die Renaissance des Christentums im 16. Jahrhundert* (Tuebingen-Leipzig, 1904), who stresses this aspect especially in Erasmus and Zwingli.

19. Kristeller, "Augustine and the Early Renaissance"; P. Polman, *L'Elément historique dans la controverse religieuse du XVI e siècle* (Gembloux, 1932).

20. U. Cassuto, *Gli Ebrei a Firenze nell 'età del rinascimento* (Florence, 1918), 275ff; S. Garofalo, "Gli umanisti italiani del secolo XV e la Bibbia," *Biblica,* XXVII (1946), 338-375.

21. Grabmann, *Die Geschichte der katholischen Theologie,* 155; L. von Pastor, *Geschichte der Päpste,* x (Freiburg, 1926), 147ff, 560ff.

22. Polman, *L'Elément historique.*

23. Grabmann, *Die Geschichte der katholischen Theologie,* 185ff.

24. Bruni, *Humanistisch-philosophische Schriften,* ed. H. Baron, 99f, 16of.

25. R. Sabbadini, *La scuola e gli studi di Guarino Guarini Veronese* (Catania, 1896), 138ff.

26. Pastor, *Geschichte der Päpste,* x, 189; Polman, *L'Elément historique,* 392ff.

27. Polman, 539ff ("A la considérer dans son orientation historique, la controverse religieuse du XVI e siècle se rattache à l'humanisme"). E. Fueter (*Geschichte der neueren Historiographie* [Munich, 1911], 246ff) misses the problem by stating that humanism ignored the church, and that ecclesiastic historiography, as a child of the Reformation, was independent of humanism.

28. F. Seebohm, *The Oxford Reformers* (London, 1887); W. Dress, *Die Mystik des Marsilio Ficino* (Berlin-Leipzig, 1929); P. A. Duhamel, "The Oxford Lectures of John Colet," *Journal of the History of Ideas,* XIV (1953), 493-510.

29. Cf. "Augustine and the Early Renaissance."

30. See ch. 1, n. 3.

31. J. B. Bury, *The Idea of Progress* (London, 1920); Richard F. Jones, *Ancient and Moderns* (St. Louis, 1936).

32. J. Burckhardt, *Weltgeschichtliche Betrachtungen* (Leipzig, 1935), 10; *Force and Freedom,* tr. James H. Nichols (New York, 1943), 86.

33. ". . . duo praecipue paranda sunt arma, cui sit . . . cum universa vitiorum cohorte pugnandum . . . precatio et scientia . . . Sed precatio quidem potior, ut quae cum Deo sermones misceat, at scientia non minus necessaria tamen." (Desiderius Erasmus, "Enchiridion militis Christiani," 1503, in his *Ausgewählte Werke,* ed. H. and A. Holborn [Munich, 1933] 29).

INDEX